Becoming a Whipple Warrior

My story from surviving to thriving

Kara S. Draper

Becoming a Whipple Warrior

Copyright © 2020 Kara S. Draper

DEDICATION

I dedicate this book to my amazing mother, Suzie, and my phenomenal children Thatcher, Callister, Berenger, and Elara. Without them, I would not have survived this journey.

TABLE OF CONTENTS

Introduction

I wanted to say a few words here about why I am writing this book. Also, thank you for buying it and reading it!! If you asked me as a child what I wanted to be when I grew up I would tell you three things. A ballerina. An Egyptologist. An Author. I did train in ballet for 14 years so kind of did that one. While I am not an Egyptologist, I did many self-assigned extra credit reports about ancient Egyptian religion and culture, as well as mummified a frog as part of a science project. So not so much that one, but I'm still fascinated by Egyptian culture and would love to plan a trip to tour Egypt. The writing though. Ahh, the writing. This was my favorite pastime, and my amazing mother would "bind" my books for me, complete with my own illustrations. I still have many of them. I filled journal after journal with stories from my imagination. I even won a creative writing contest in 3rd grade and was beyond excited to get to meet one of my favorite authors, Lois Lowry! As I got older, I found less time for writing, but still longed to be a writer. I started doubting that I had anything to say that anyone would care about. I stepped completely away from it for a long time. Then I discovered blogging and began to document my life, my children, and some random short stories as well. I still dreamed of being a published author, but again self-doubt crept in and crowded out my ambitions and passions. When I finally escaped an extremely abusive marriage, I again went back to my long-time desire to be an author. This time as a way to make much needed additional income. I kept getting stuck thinking I didn't have anything to say that anyone cared about. I got overwhelmed with the time writing a book would take. More doubts about it not being perfect. After a lot of therapy and more healing (still working on things!) I decided this was something I needed to do. I realized that I have survived several lifetimes worth of things, and that I do indeed have a plethora of stories to share. Still stuck at the excuse of time, I remembered my blogs. One of the huge stories of my life is surviving an insane surgery that has profoundly changed my entire life. And I do mean everything! So, here I am, laying myself bare and sharing my blogs (with some things written after the fact the fill in some gaps) with you. It is my most sincere desire that my story helps even just one person. If you are about to have a Whipple, have had one, are a caregiver, or even a doctor, I hope this provides some interesting perspective. I had a lot of trouble finding any stories more than a few paragraphs about the experience. I am hoping that sharing this will shed a little light about just one person's experience. I hope it makes you laugh, cry, hope, and even gives you some practical advice like the importance of toddler pillows to prop your IV arm on to help you sleep. This won't be perfect. I am certain you will find typos, incorrect grammar, poor flow, and improper use of tenses. But I can promise you that this is 100% my story in all of its raw glory. The vast majority of this was written in the moment of each experience. Some of this was dictated into notepad on my phone while I was in the hospital. Some of this was playing catchup after being totally down for the count for weeks on end. It's my story of survival and perseverance and I am sharing it with you.

The Beginning Part

What is a "Whipple?"

A Whipple procedure, also known as a pancreaticoduodenectomy, is an extremely complex procedure. The name comes from Dr. Allen Whipple, a Columbia University surgeon who was the first to perform the operation in 1935. The name is a lot more fun sounding than the procedure itself!!

During this procedure the head of the pancreas is removed, along with the first part of the small intestines (duodenum), gallbladder, bile duct, and in some cases the bottom of the stomach including (or not) the pyloric valve. It's an open surgery (I have a 7-8" vertical incision scar that I'm super proud of!) that can take 4-12 hours. Mine took about 7-8 hours.

Needless to say, this is an extraordinarily complex and dangerous surgery. Not something anyone takes lightly and you absolutely need a specialized and highly experienced surgeon for this one.

Being an historically healthy woman in her early 40s, a Whipple was not exactly on my life plan. In fact, up until February of the "year of my whipple" I had no medical history to speak of, and had no clue what a pancreas even does. For the record, it produces insulin and the digestive enzymes needed to digest fats, carbs, and proteins. Pretty important. It's also nestled way back behind the stomach so super tricky to even get to!

So, how did I end up a "Whipple Warrior?" No, it was not

for attention or so I'd have material for a book. I also did not have a Whipple so I could take advantage of the kindness of my friends who pitched in to help my family as I recovered. And no, it was no so people could "waste" their prayers on me. Though my ex-husband has said all of these things to me. Repeatedly. But I digress...

Through my abusive marriage I gained a lot of weight. I do mean a LOT of weight. By 2018, after 10 years of marriage and 4 children I had ballooned up to 315 lbs. I am 5'6" so that's pretty huge. I saw zero value in myself and gained weight as a defense mechanism of sorts.

By 2018 my daughter was 2 and becoming more aware of things around her. I realized that I needed to start valuing myself and setting a better example for her, and my boys. Something in me just clicked and I just decided it was "time" and started my weight loss journey on January 1, 2018. The journey was really more about healing myself and caring for myself than it was about food and exercise.

Long story short, I lost the weight all naturally by focusing on one small change at a time and being very consistent with it. I began by simply not snacking after dinner anymore. I averaged about 10 lbs of loss per month so aggressive but not unhealthy. By the end of the 2018 I was down 140 lbs!

One thing I did not know as I began my journey back to health was that losing a large amount of weight relatively quickly can lead to gallbladder issues. So ultimately, putting myself first, beginning to heal, and losing weight quite literally saved my life. As you will read in the upcoming chapters, had it not been for my crapped-out gallbladder needing to be removed, my ampullory adenoma would not have been found and I never would have had this live saving (and changing!) surgery!

From Ironman to Whipple Warrior

Early February, 2019 - I started my Saturday full of excitement at the thought of officially kicking off my Ironman training. I was down about 160 lbs at this point and felt like I finally had my life back. I was healthy, fit, and full of energy. I planned to take my two oldest boys with me to the bike shop to get my new bike and have it tuned up.

I had started experiencing distinct pain Thursday evening after dinner (shrimp with avocado, sushi, and roasted brussels sprouts and carrots with one chocolate covered strawberry). The pain was significant, but not overwhelming. It was about the same as I'd been experiencing most times after eating lately. This had been going on for the past 6 months or so, but I'd been ignoring it as not significant. The pain was under my ribs on the right side and radiated to my back. Imagine wearing a SUPER tight band just under your breasts...it was a squeezing type of pain that did not let up.

I winced and wheezed my way to get the bike. I didn't even get fully dressed or put on any makeup. I wasn't feeling well. I thought it would pass. I thought I was just feeling "full" from the few steamed veggie dumplings I had for lunch. Fullness does not feel like this did, but hey, hindsight is 20/20! I was damned if I was going to miss my bike though! Not my smartest move, but honestly if I hadn't been out already, I may not have gone anywhere at all so this trip, in a way, helped save my life.

I met my friend to get the bike and we waited for the tune-up. I was feeling worse and worse and couldn't stand up straight. By the time they got to my bike I was squatting on the ground and could barely stand. I'm just stubborn enough that I made it through getting the bike tuned up.

As we were leaving the bike shop, I told the boys they'd need to come to an urgent care with me. I was barely able to stand the pain at this point and knew I could not make the whole drive home. When we pulled out, I saw the big blue "H" sign and thought, yup, I need a full Emergency Room. It took only about 5 minutes to get there and the pain was excruciating by the time we got there. I was seen pretty quickly and nearly passed out on the floor from the pain as I was being triaged in.

They rushed me to ultrasound as they immediately suspected gallstones. They also asked me to get the boys picked up because they didn't want kids in a hospital during flu season. I only found out later that they wanted them taken care of because they thought I might be in emergency surgery soon. My ultrasound showed a gallbladder full of stones as well as swelling in the bile duct which is indicative of a gallbladder squeezing out a stone that gets stuck there. Though they didn't see an actual stone in the ducts.

I had a bunch of blood drawn for labs and found out that my liver enzymes were quite elevated (2-3 times over the top end of normal). At this point my blood pressure also tanked to 89/52. That got me all kinds of attention! It eventually went back up. At this point the boys were picked up and I planned to drive myself home when I was released. I was admitted shortly after the boys left and I never did get to drive home. I was told I needed an MRI to confirm if I had a stone in my bile duct. Apparently, a stone stuck in the bile duct is an emergency.

I finally saw a surgical resident who gave the go ahead for the MRI. He also talked to me about my high liver enzymes and decided to run a lot more blood work. He was "intrigued" with my clinical presentation, history, and labs. The MRI showed no lodged stone and looked fairly good.

The surgeon came in to talk to me and that is when I learned that if he had only seen the ultrasounds, he would have operated on me immediately just based on those images. They were that bad. Kudos to the team for keeping their cool? Since the MRI looked ok, it meant I was not emergent, but was still clearly having issues.

At this point, I got passed over to gastroenterology. I then spent my first ever night in the hospital, connected to an IV and trying to sleep while getting vitals monitored frequently and still in a lot of pain.

A quick word on pain. My tolerance for pain is extraordinarily high. As a natural redhead, this is a genetic trait (on the MC1R gene), along with needing about 25% more anesthesia than "normal" people. Here are a few things I've experienced with no pain:

- ➢ Natural childbirth. 4 times. I do not have dainty babies either! My first was 7 lbs 13 oz (a month early!), My second was 8 lbs 8oz, my third was 9 lbs 9 oz, and my fourth was a whopping 11 lbs 1 oz. I delivered that last one in a blow up tub in my bathroom.
- ➢ A torn tendon in my hip. I was not even aware it was torn until I had an MRI for another hip issue and it was discovered. I'm currently living with 2 severe labral tears in my hips.
- ➢ 2 broken feet. I actually completed a half ironman with these two broken feet. I only thought I needed a good foot massage.

I saw the gastro, the incredible Dr. Kamil Obideen, who determined that I DID have a stone in my bile duct on the ultrasound, but that it had passed on its own by the time I had the MRI. This is apparently what caused my liver enzymes to spike. He felt this was still surgical though. He wanted more labs to confirm and if he was right, my liver enzymes should be coming down. The next lab draw was too soon to see a change and the enzymes were still on the rise – scary! By the next lab draw, they are coming down.

At this point I am just sitting in a hospital bed, bored, and googling everything. I start thinking maybe I can avoid the surgery and manage it with the timing and volume of foods I eat. I was already following a gallbladder friendly diet so no big changes coming there. Low sugars, low carbs, healthy fats, but still on the low end of fats.

I was finally cleared to have a meal! It was Sunday night and I had not eaten since Saturday early morning and with the pain finally under control I was starving. Hospital food is just awful and pretty much only offers sugars, gluten, dairy, fats, and sodium...so drumming up more business there! My fantastic nurse suggested Grub Hub so I ordered a nice, fresh salad with some seared tuna. No dressings. Pretty much the best, healthiest thing I could have had. Or so I thought.

It was delicious and I felt revived both physically and mentally. Until 20 minutes later when I started having more of the same severe gallbladder and liver pain that brought me in. I needed IV pain meds because I hit the point where the pain was so bad it was making it incredibly hard to breathe. That episode convinced me that regardless of any future side effects or restrictions, I needed my gallbladder out ASAP. I could not eat anything without debilitating pain.

The next morning, Monday, I had another scary blood pressure episode where it dropped to 76/42. Terrifyingly low. One nurse sat me up and another nurse squeezed a full bag of fluids into me as hard and as fast as she could. Things were intense. My pulse was in the low 40s. After about 30 min it was back up to around 95/50, so out of the danger zone. After that I got some of my labs back and my liver enzymes were still going down, confirming that I did have a stone in my bile duct.

I finally saw the surgical team again and everyone agreed

that I need surgery. The option was to wait until Tuesday (the next day) because the OR was already booked for the day or go home and schedule for next week. Except I cannot eat anything without severe pain so yeah, having surgery tomorrow!

Now, I wait, and I nap. Hungry.

My First Surgery: Cholecystectomy

I made it all the way to age 42 with no real medical history and no surgeries. The wait from Monday afternoon to Tuesday morning for my surgery felt like forever. I was so nervous and had no idea what to expect.

I did have a very welcome surprise distraction though. My cousin, Anne, was in town from Paris for the night and came to visit me. My mother had also driven down from North Carolina to be with me as soon as she learned about the impending surgery. My Mom, Suzie, is also a nurse so the perfect medical advocate and caretaker!

I had been brought up to a bigger room to await my surgery and was told I should be able to go home a few hours after the surgery. I was able to take a shower after several days without one and felt refreshed. I could not bring myself to eat actual food but managed a few sips of the worst broth you can imagine. While just a home cook, I am darned good at it and since I make my own broth, this was extra disappointing. Fun Fact! I had auditioned for Master Chef in 2018 and Chef Ramsey's team loved my food and I made it to casting before pulling out due to the time commitment.

Surgery was scheduled for early in the morning and I did not sleep much. Besides the nerves, there was an IV in my arm, nurses coming in every few hours to check my vitals, and the team that draws blood for labs comes in around 4 am. Hospitals have apparently never seen or heard Daniel Tiger say, "when you're sick, rest is best, rest is best!"

The morning of the surgery I was rolled down to the pre-op area and talked to before being pumped full of "relaxing" drugs. They do indeed relax you! I was not a bit nervous by the time I was rolled into the OR. I was not awake or aware for very long once in the OR, but I distinctly remember my last thought being that the room looked cluttered and that they would benefit greatly from a "5S" makeover.

I spent a couple of years as a safety professional and 5S is a workplace organizational method that uses a list of 5 Japanese words that translate to: Sort, Set in Order, Shine, Standardize, and Sustain.

The surgery itself was uneventful with no complications...until there were. At this point the only aggravating thing was that the surgeon was supposed to do something with contrast while he was in there to confirm there was no bile duct obstruction. He did not do this. He said he looked and did not see anything concerning so just didn't do it. This was a major error, but in hindsight a huge stroke of luck!

Back Home!

I was home by dinnertime on the same day as my surgery. The pain meds wore off and I was extremely uncomfortable. While I could walk, it was terribly slow. Like a geriatric sloth on an unwilling outing.

The most painful part was sitting and standing. The transitions. I was ok once I was down and ok once I was up. The in between part? Not so much. I was bound and determined to recover quickly and get back on track with my Ironman training! So stubborn. So naïve...I am nothing if not an eternal optimist.

Eating was slow going, but without the pain I had been experiencing for so long. "Meals" consisted of half a slice of turkey lunchmeat, 3 blueberries, and one slice of cucumber. This took me ages to eat and still made me so nervous.

I was feeling well enough to have a visitor on day 2 of being home. As I was chatting with my friend, I started feeling unwell again. Cold, clammy, flushed, weak, eyes glazing over, and the pain was coming back. I tried to ride it out but finally told my friend I thought I needed a nap.

I made it to the bedroom to try and sleep it off. At this point I was thinking that I had just overdone it by sitting for too long and trying to "entertain." The pain escalated quickly. Within a few hours it was unbearable, and I was having a hard time taking a breath. My mom called the surgeon for me and we were told it was "normal" and see him in his office on Monday. This was Thursday. I was in such excruciating pain that I am breathing very shallow and could not move. I clearly needed to get back to the ER. I could not even imagine getting to, much less sitting in a car though.

Enter ambulance ride #1! 911 was called and I was removed from my bed by the paramedics and strapped to a stretcher. The paramedic, who were wonderful, also managed to track red Georgia clay all over my light colored, and nearly new bedroom carpet. I was alert enough to notice this because I am my mother's daughter – ha!

The other thing I was painfully aware of during this time was that my children had to see an ambulance, lights flashing, arrive at their house to take their mother out of her room and away to the hospital. My heart shattered thinking about how scary, confusing, and stressful this was for my babies. At the time they were 3, 5, 6, and 8.

I have to say, ambulance rides are not so fun. Getting a needle poked in your arm for an IV while strapped to a locked down gurney in a vehicle with zero suspension while traveling on bumpy roads is...alarming. Luckily, I was in so much pain that was the least of my concerns.

I was being taken to the hospital closest to me, which is a much better hospital than where my surgery was performed. I will say that one benefit of arriving at in ER via ambulance is that you go directly into a room. No waiting! Gotta find those silver linings! It is like the red carpet of hospitals that you hope you never need to use.

My mother went with me, so I was not alone. Since the IV had already been started they were able to get a big dose of morphine on board relatively quickly. Morphine does not work well for me and it only just barley took the edge off the pain. I was so scared and confused about why I was feeling like this after a surgery that was supposed to have fixed me.

I had another CAT scan and labs and was thrilled to see Dr. Obideen, the GI doctor who helped me in the ER a few days ago by figuring out the issue and insisting on surgery. The CAT scan confirmed a totally obstructed bile duct, and I was admitted and scheduled for an ERCP (endoscopic retrograde cholangiopancreatography) the following day. I had no idea what this was but soon learned it was a procedure where they put a camera down your throat to look at the liver, gallbladder, and pancreas. I was suitably terrified.

Naturally, I did what anyone would do and googled as much as I could and proceeded to freak myself out. Completely unnecessary, but I had nothing else to do.

The procedure was complete in under an hour and Dr. Obideen had to cut open my bile duct to drain "sludge" that was completely blocking it. Remember when my mother asked the surgeon if he'd checked for a bile duct blockage and he said no because everything looked good? Turns out, it was not so good. That was an egregious mistake to make. I would be mad about it, except it ended up saving my life.

Since I had shared with Dr. Obideen a lot about my weight loss, diet history, and issues I'd been having with gluten, I'd asked about the celiac biopsy since he'd be in there. I was full of pain meds and thought the conversation went a little different than it actually did. Stay tuned for the plot twist on this one!

I ended up needing to spend another night in the hospital to ensure the procedure did not cause pancreatitis, which is a risk of the ERCP. I did fine and was able to head home the next day.

My follow-up with Dr. Obideen was 3 weeks away.

Food Anxiety

While I no longer have gallbladder pain after eating, I am still having a LOT of issues eating. I have got an appointment with my gastroenterologist on Tuesday. I am also waiting on test results for food allergy/intolerance, environmental, histamine, and some other digestive stuff. That is an "unofficial" test I found online that uses hair samples. I am eager to figure out why I'm still having issues.

I will get the celiac biopsy results back Tuesday with my GI. Regardless of if that comes back positive or not, I know I need to completely avoid gluten. Not to be trendy or as part of any kind of diet that restricts carbs, but because they make me feel so sick. For the record, I do not avoid carbs, but my carbs are primarily from veggies and fruits.

Here is a sample of what is happening EVERY SINGLE TIME I eat anything either with gluten or that has been cross contaminated with gluten:

- ➢ Bloating/distended stomach (seriously look 6 months pregnant!)
- ➢ Swelling (especially my hands and face)
- ➢ Joint pain, muscle pain, and inflammation
- ➢ Feeling flushed/hot
- ➢ Headache
- ➢ Sour stomach
- ➢ Belching, gas, and cramping

➤ Mental fogginess

➤ Itching

➤ Mystery rashes

➤ Anxiety

Sometimes the symptoms start quickly, but often it takes a few hours to start feeling the effects. Then it builds and builds and lasts for days to a week or more. It is horrible. I accidentally had an exceedingly small amount of gluten on Tuesday and by Saturday was almost recovered from it when I had a cross contamination incident over dinner last night. I currently feel like death warmed over and I am using talk to text for this because my face is so swollen it is hard to see.

Gluten is not the only thing giving me an issue. Often, I will have remarkably similar reactions, though they are not quite as extreme as with gluten, to other foods. The problem is it seems like I have at least some level of reaction to everything that I eat, and I cannot pinpoint the specific cause. I eat EXCEPTIONALLY clean and almost exclusively whole foods.

The list of things I do not react to at all seems to be limited to plain sliced turkey breast, blueberries, cucumber, lemon, ginger, tea, water, and coffee. Add anything else, or even have more than an ounce or so of any of those foods (liquids I can handle in any amount!) at a time and I start reacting. Pretty much the very act of eating will cause me to bloat immediately.

It is not normal and not ok. It also causes a great deal of anxiety around food and a lot of awkward social situations. For example, I am currently trying to figure out how to explain why I will not be eating over a lunch meeting that I have planned for tomorrow. I know that this gluten attack is a bad one and is going to last at least a week and I am terrified of adding anything else into my system that could make it worse. I just want to feel OK!!

I have spent an incredible number of years explaining away these constellations of symptoms. I even went to a doctor for it about 4 years ago. I was completely dismissed due to my weight, which was high at the time. Oh yeah, size discrimination in the medical field is real! If you are being dismissed, find a new doctor who will listen to you. After my gallbladder experience and realizing that had I paid attention to my symptoms sooner I may have been able to resolve the situation without surgery, I did not want that to happen again.

If anyone else is having these types of symptoms, I would encourage you to go talk to a gastroenterologist or an allergist and try to figure out what is going on. For me, I suspect that the issues they found with my liver when they were doing testing for my gallbladder have something to do with this. I feel like a patient from the show HOUSE with a weird set of symptoms and lab results that do not have one clear answer and solution. Hopefully, I will get some answers soon!

The BIG Diagnosis

Good news! I have a PRE-cancerous Ampullary Adenoma in my bile duct that will need to be surgically removed.

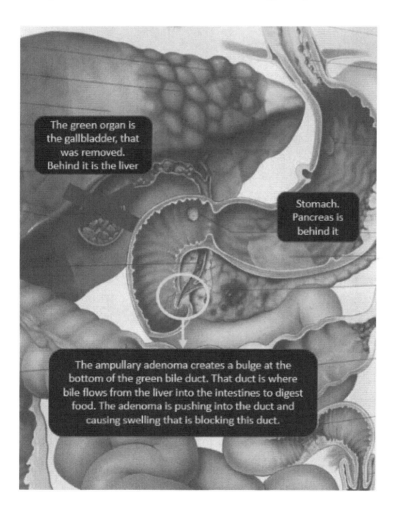

The green organ is the gallbladder, that was removed. Behind it is the liver

Stomach. Pancreas is behind it

The ampullary adenoma creates a bulge at the bottom of the green bile duct. That duct is where bile flows from the liver into the intestines to digest food. The adenoma is pushing into the duct and causing swelling that is blocking this duct.

There are a few reasons I am claiming this as incredibly GOOD news. But before we get there let me just add that the minute I heard 'cancerous' I missed the 'pre' part. My mind just went blank. I was also stunned because I had thought I was coming in to get the results of a celiac test. As it turns out, Dr. Obideen had seen a swollen area, in a place you are absolutely expecting it to be swollen given the blockage I had, and decided to do a biopsy just to be sure. Amazing instinct!

Back to why this is such good news...

First, it is pre-cancerous. Emphasis on PRE!!

Second, it finally explains all my symptoms and issues with eating. The adenoma is causing the swelling in the bile duct which is blocking the flow of bile which makes it painful when I eat because there is no bile to digest the food.

Third, this result means it is most likely the volume of food increasing that has caused the issues as opposed to any food intolerances. Anything more than, for example, 4 blueberries, 1 thin slice of cucumber, and 1 thinly sliced piece of deli turkey, and all the symptoms flare up.

Fourth, it is a relatively 'easy' fix with surgery. (HAHAHAHAHA - famous last words!!) It is yet to be determined if I will have a procedure in advance of the surgery to add a stent into the bile duct so I can digest food. That will depend on how soon we can get surgery scheduled.

Fifth, it is incredibly fortunate that we even found it because this type of thing is typically asymptomatic and only found if you happen to be having an endoscopic procedure for something else and they see it. I am also apparently "WAY too young for this."

If I had not lost the weight that I did, which caused my gallbladder issue, we never would have found this. So, for me, losing the weight truly did just save my life in a very real sense.

Dr. Obideen called the surgeon, Dr. Eddie Abdalla, when I was in the room with him and is faxing over my records over to him straight away. Dr. Abdalla is the absolute best in the area and specializes in issues like mine and surgeries like this. I had more labs drawn (liver function, as he suspects my liver enzymes are still up due to continued blockage, and the hereditary hemochromatosis test because my father had hemochromatosis which causes a toxic buildup of iron), and he is going to call me personally the minute the results come back. I have called to make an appointment with the surgeon to discuss options and the path forward and am waiting on the call back from scheduling.

As I understand it right now, the surgical approach would be preferred (cut that shit all the way out!!), but there is also an alternative that is newer and more specialized. It is an endoscopic procedure that does carry a little bit higher risk of side effects and there is also only one guy who even does it. While I do not have my exact path forward, I am working to get it figured out as quickly as possible and get treated as aggressively as possible.

What Really Happens When I Eat?

I thought I would do a quick recap to show the reality of what's happening every time I eat and why it's so uncomfortable.

I get extreme bloating that looks like I am 6-7 months pregnant, as well as some awful swelling, mostly my hands and face. It makes me extremely sick to my stomach, I get crampy, gassy, feverish, headache, and feel generally very unwell. This is caused by the continued obstruction of my bile duct. I have got very little bile that's able to flow through and aid with digestion. So, the food just sits there. I do take digestive enzymes, but it takes several days of pushing water (often lemon water and ginger water) along with herbal teas with dandelion root, chamomile, and turmeric to flush it through.

I have an appointment with the surgeon, Dr. Abdalla, tomorrow morning. On my birthday – way to start the day! I am hoping to come out with an action plan and surgery scheduled. I am not sure how the appointment will really go though. As I understand it there are a few different surgical options and the doctor needs to determine the best course.

People keep asking how I am doing. I keep saying I am fine. I am good. I am staying positive. That is all true. I am also scared and nervous and am having a lot of anxiety. I worry about how fast this type of pre-cancerous things can turn to cancer and I am hyper aware that this was from a biopsy 3 weeks ago and is that how long it takes? I am trying to keep my mind otherwise occupied though so I've ordered a cute hospital gown and my own grippy socks so at least I can be cute for this surgery – HAHA! I am totally going to monogram my gown. Not sure if that means I am super "basic" or super "extra." I am old enough that I'm not even sure the difference.

In any case, writing about it helps so I will keep the blog updated as I learn new news and get a plan together. Mom is going to come down to help with the kids again and I am grateful that this time, the surgery will be planned!

Met with the Surgeon for my Birthday!

Not how I expected to kick off my birthday – 43 is starting with a BANG!!

My surgeon is amazing, and I feel 1000% confident that he is both the best and the best for me! It is a serious and very specialized surgery that is open (versus laparoscopic), lasts 3-4 hours, and I will be in the hospital 5-6 days. But prognosis is good and I should bounce back pretty quickly! (again, HAHAHAHAHA, famous last words!)

Prior to the surgery they're having me get a colonoscopy to be sure there's nothing else we need to address, since the digestive system is all connected and this adenoma makes me more likely to have colon issues.

I also met with a nutritionist and have an appointment with a geneticist to help figure out possible causes and to inform a follow up plan. As for nutrition she let me know that I am already doing everything she would recommend so I'll keep that up. I will meet with her again during pre-op to discuss the post-surgical plan. The only concern right now, obviously, is that I am not able to eat anywhere near enough. But I won't be able to eat any more until surgery so I'm doing the best I can to get in the best nutrition I can, especially protein. Today, I weighed in at 149 and will likely keep losing until surgery.

The plan is to get all of this done in the next 2 weeks. Still working on scheduling. My Mom will also be coming down again to help. It is an odd feeling to be NOT wanting to lose any more weight. I actually starting to feel more boney than I'd like. Hell of a way to finish off a weight loss journey!

I got my pre surgery labs scheduled as well as my pre surgical visit with my surgeon

I kind of freaked out at the labs visit. First, they registered me for the stay. No payment due...I have hit all my insurance limits already! Then I meet with the anesthesiologist. Blood pressure, pulse, listen to heart and lungs, and look in my mouth to assess if the breathing tube will fit (it will). She starts describing the drugs they will use and throws out there about an epidural and I'm like, excuse me, what? This is how I learn that I will be getting what amounts to an IV directly in my spine so I can have a constant supply of pain meds (fentanyl) for 2-5 DAYS post-surgery to help control the pain. I will apparently need to push the "booster" button for extra meds before I need to do things like move for vitals or get up to pee.

This is when I realized I have completely and totally underestimated this surgery and recovery. Open surgery is not even in the same ballpark as laparoscopic surgery.

Next up, bloodwork. Like a super lot of blood!! I ask what the labs are, and nurse rattles them off and casually throws in one for a 'cancer marker.' I am all, wait what? Back up. What is that test because I need to google the hell out of it! If you care to google it is the CA 19-9. It is a test for pancreatic cancer. Boom. Game changer...and my first question for the surgeon at my appointment tomorrow. I mean I get why they are doing it, but holy shitballs Batman, this just got a whole new level of real.

My brain is shutdown. I let my manager and my team know that I'm pretty much out now and gave them the list of the last few things I need them to pick up for me, so no balls drop while I'm out...who knows, for all of April? I may go in some if I need the distraction, and I very well might. I can just no longer reliably commit to anything.

The Colonoscopy – LOOK AWAY!

I have been very on the fence about sharing this. I know I am always very transparent and open about what is going on with me, but holy cow, this one is both very personal as well as horrifyingly, and hilariously, embarrassing. I mean, completely mortifying. I may not look anyone in the eye every again.

That being said, a colonoscopy is something everyone has once they hit 50, and many have them a lot sooner. It is a critical screening and can help prevent colon cancer. Prevention is KEY so please, schedule one. Also, Katie Couric had one on TV so no excuses! So, in the spirit of sharing, normalizing, and preparing anyone who may have one coming up, here is how it all went down. Also, after a profoundly serious day (scroll to the previous post for that), I thought some levity was in order!

WARNING *Go to the bathroom now or you might just pee a little from laughter. It is completely ridiculous.*

The Prep Protocol

1:50 pm: extra credit pre-protocol poop! I always have

been an overachiever

2:00 pm: The protocol begins! Took 2 5mg Dulcolax with a glass of water

2:00 – 3:00 pm: redecorated the family room with 2 new rugs. Threw in a deep clean for good measure since all the furniture is moved!

3:00 pm: some ominous tummy rumbling, but nothing yet

3:10 – 3:25 pm: start preparing 2 loaves of bread. I bake weekly and we have not purchased bread in over a year (even though I cannot tolerate gluten, my kids love it)

3:30 pm: first poop. Totally normal and uneventful.

3:45 pm: Post surgery new TV is set up in our bedroom. Nurses thank you baskets are nearly complete. The 'mattress genie' has also just arrived!

4:00 pm: I am warned to "get myself a seatbelt" because this is going to "send me into orbit." Noted. Seatbelt procured

4:30 – 5:00 pm: got bread ready and shaped for rise #2. Fed dogs and cleaned up dog pee that was dangerously close to my brand spanking new rug!

5:00 pm: tummy is rumbling, and stage 2 has begun! MiraLAX mixed into organic coconut water. 8 oz every 15 min until I've had half (approx. 32 oz!)

5:25 pm: finished the first quart of the MiraLAX drink! Round 1 is done!! Round 2 begins at 8 pm

6:00 pm: got bread in the oven...took it out 35 min later. 2 perfect loaves!

6:43 pm: Poop at last! Poop at last! Thank god almighty, I have pooped at last! I was beginning to think I would be the first person ever NOT to poop during "the protocol." Feeling a little crampy, but not too bad...yet?

6:45 pm: the dam has broken, and full cleansing has begun!

7:00 pm: I have lit 3 candles and a stick of incense. I have also locked the bedroom door and am considering if we have hazmat tape for outside the door.

7:05 pm: I believe I am empty. I do not understand how round 2 can proceed without shitting out an internal organ

7:15 pm: I feel totally fine and normal. 45 minutes until round 2 begins

7:30 pm: more "cleansing" prior to round 2...100% liquid!

7:56 pm: liquid is pouring from my bum like rain. Florida afternoon storm rain, not Seattle rain.

8:00 pm: round 2 has begun. 2 more 5mg Dulcolax down the hatch! Tummy is still rumbling

8:30 pm: I shat on the floor. 2 feet from the toilet. I was running. I was so close. I fell short. Dear God, make it stop.

I have not even started the next round of MiraLAX. Oh my god, I am scared for the next few hours

8:40 pm: had to take a shower

8:54 pm: started round 2 of the god forsaken MiraLAX drink. Mentally this last round is hard. I know too much now.

9:15 pm: having trouble drinking the MiraLAX. My body just doesn't want to!!!! It is dribbling down the sides of my mouth as I try to drink it. I am vaguely nauseated.

9:43 pm MiraLAX drink is done!! I think I've just ruined coconut water forever. It used to be my favorite. I should have thought ahead better.

9:50 pm: Apparently there is a beach in my colon? Was that sand with the water? What is happening?!

10:05 pm: I think I might just sleep on the toilet. It is hard to run and clench at the same time. And all these years I thought I was good at multitasking. I am not. It is a problem

10:16 pm: Still sitting on the toilet. The seat is hard, but I am afraid to move.

10:27 pm: reluctantly getting up now. Both of my feet have fallen asleep

10:29 pm: just kidding! I am back. In the nick of time. This afternoon I was proud that I got the living room redecorated and made bread. Tonight, I'm proud that I didn't just shit my pants. Again.

10:32 pm: There is nothing left, yet there is still more. How? What? From where?!

11:05 pm: I am exhausted and still shooting out straight liquid. I am going to sleep so, so much tomorrow! I am honestly afraid to go to bed. My stomach is still rumbling and making so much noise!

11:13 pm: I have laid out leggings and a cozy sweater to wear to the colonoscopy tomorrow. I packed my pink polka dot hospital gown that I monogrammed. I just want to sleep, alas, here I am, back on the toilet. It is slowing down. I think I'm nearly done, and I believe I've achieved a "clean colon." The instructions indicate that to achieve the desired result you will be peeing urine or tea colored liquid from your bum. Achieved.

11:17 pm: Nope. Not empty yet!

11:27 pm: still going. I am so confused. And tired. I must leave the house at 6 am

12:02 am: I have gone through nearly a full roll of toilet paper. I am done. About to attempt to sleep for a few hours. I am putting a maxi pad in the back of my underpants. You can never be too careful. The bed had white sheets and I would like to keep them that way!

12:11 am: back on my throne. Apparently, I will not be sleeping tonight

12:33 am: still not sleeping. I am so exhausted I feel sick

1:53 am: bathroom. Very little. I am thirsty but cannot drink

2:00 am: I finally sleep. Reluctantly and fearfully

The morning of my Colonoscopy!

5:25 am: I appear to have survived!! What a way to wake up through. Tummy is still rumbling and I am still peeing from my bum. I am not sure I'll ever recover from this.

5:34 am: total 24-hour weight loss from the protocol is 4.7 lbs. Just took the best shower of my life! I smell tropical and am happily slathered in a delightful mixture of cocoa butter and coconut oil

5:44 am: tummy is still far too noisy

5:58 am: I am off! Since there was absolutely no way of getting the kids up dressed and out of the house by 6 AM to get me there by seven, I am driving myself there and will leave my car there overnight and go back for it in the morning. There was just no other way. It is very strange to be getting in the car without coffee! I will have to hit a Starbucks on the ride home!!

6:32 am: no traffic so I am here super early. I would always rather be early than late. I will sit in my warm car listening to my audiobook

6:45 – 8:30 am: Checked in, vitals checked, IV started, rolled across in the bed to the procedure room, took a nap and it was over. I was aware of nothing. I remember nothing.

9:05 Colonoscopy is all done. I got to wear my pink polka dot monogrammed gown and grippy pink bunny socks. Had a great nap! Looking forward to more napping all day. Everything looks good. They removed 1 un-concerning polyp. So happy this part is over and done!

10:00 am: home and had some turkey, blueberries, and a string cheese to start slowly refilling my system. I am not ravenously hungry as everyone seems to advise I would be, but I'm guessing that is because I haven't been eating much anyway so my body is used to being relatively empty.

12:36 pm: had a great nap! My tummy continues to rumble, but at this point it is all bark and no bite. I feel generally gassy and full of air, but not uncomfortable at all. The plan is to rest the rest of the day, but I am already planning to refinish a smaller dresser later this afternoon if I can!

1:13 pm: ok the all bark and no bite thing...the bite part is back. Wondering if I will ever poop solid again.

2:57 pm: goodness, my stomach is still rumbling like crazy!!

My tummy rumbled for the rest of the day and I was tooting out the air the pumped in for the procedure all day. No "sharts" though, so that was a win! Tummy continued to be a bit rumbly the next day as well, but much less. As I had read, the prep was the hardest/longest part and the procedure itself was no big deal. My next colonoscopy will be in 5 years.

The End

My Final Pre-Op Visit

I got to my pre op visit too early. It is spring break week so I am pretty sure the whole state of GA just up and shifted down to FL. For those of us left here to hold down the fort, traffic is confusingly amazing. It was so clear yesterday that I questioned if I was taking Elara to school and heading to work on a Sunday. Same situation today – no traffic! But, because it's Atlanta and traffic is always unpredictable, I still had to leave early 'just in case.' This post will be a record of my thoughts in real time that I will post later.

So, here I sit. Waiting. The nurse checked me into a room and took my vitals. I am 147.8 lbs so despite not being able to eat much, I'm maintaining pretty-well (I was 149 at my last visit on 3/22)! Then he went out to 'check on my labs' which I had done yesterday at 4 pm. I am at a 9 am appointment so talk about a quick turnaround. I am a ball of nerves. I wrote down all my questions (mom helped!) and I will voice record the meeting again so I can go back over it in case my brain shuts down.

I was just handed a cancer support community packet of information. No info, no words, nothing. A nurse came in, handed it to me and told me to look through this because they were some great programs that I could take advantage of. What the what??? But I do not have cancer...

There next person in the room was a physician's assistant. I immediately asked, "do I have cancer?" He said yes. Wait. What?? What, what the what?!! I explained that this was

47

news to me and that I'd only been told I have an ampullory adenoma that was PRE-cancerous. He said he thought it was a carcinoma. Ok, please check that!! He checked as he was speaking and the words he chose included that I may have a small round of chemo after surgery 'to be sure.'

EXCUSE ME?!! Then he finds it in my chart. "Oh, you're right. It's just an adenoma and it's pre-cancerous. Not cancer. You don't have cancer." HOLY SHIT! Gee, do you think that is the kind of thing you might want to check before speaking with a patient who is already nervous before surgery??!!!?? He ended up being amazing through the rest of my experience so it was all ok.

Though what they've found (so far) is PRE-cancerous, I am functionally being treated as a cancer patient since the treatment (i.e. surgery) is basically the same. The surgeon confirmed that I do NOT have cancer and that even if it was cancer, that the treatment for early cancer is still JUST the surgery, no chemo.

After speaking with my surgeon (totally brought him some jelly/jam I made to distract myself from the upcoming surgery!) and learned a few things. I will be off work for a full month. There is a small chance my ampullectomy will convert to a full Whipple (At this point, I only remember learning about it on Grey's Anatomy. She died.) There is also a chance that when the more detailed pathology comes back they might need to open me back up and do the full Whipple (if they don't get sufficient margins, etc.).

Obviously, the hope and most likely scenario is that the ampullectomy is all that is needed and that it will fully resolve all of my eating issues as expected. Further, there is also a chance that if this surgery does not resolve all of my eating and digestion issues, they may still need to go back a few months down the road to do the full Whipple. Even though Whipple is super fun to say, I really do not want it. This surgery is already a big deal, but the Whipple is even more so.

Sounds like the epidural for pain management is amazing though! By reducing/controlling pain, it both speeds healing as well as helps to reduce the infection rate. Good stuff! I will also be able to "boost" with IV meds if needed.

Interesting fact. The tipping point when complications from ampullectomy start to significantly decline is when a hospital does more than one per MONTH (I think I mentioned before how rare this is!). My surgeon does 5-7 per WEEK! Again, I am so incredibly grateful to have one of the best surgeons in the world at this procedure. The reason he does that many is that people travel from all over just for him. He is basically a surgical God!

Just spoke to the dietitian/nutritionist. Before and after surgery I will be on clear liquids only. Oh, and I get to do another mini bowel prep. Nowhere near as intense the colonoscopy prep, but I am still not excited about it.

That one polyp, by the way was a tubular polyp that was pre-cancerous but is extremely slow growing and not a concern. All my other labs, including my liver enzymes, were completely normal and looked fantastic. I learned that the ampullory adenoma, when it spreads, most often correlates with a colon cancer so that was what they were ruling out with the colonoscopy. Good to know and happy that was cleared!

Back to the diet. After a day or so on clear liquids it expands to any liquids. Then I progress, slowly, to the "GI diet" which is low fiber and soft foods like yogurt, eggs, soft cooked veggies, and eventually meats/fish. It expands after 4-6 weeks.

I am being kept gluten free and low dairy (causes bloating) until I am completely healed and eating normally with no pain. Then we will test slowly with gluten to confirm if I'm still reactive it. I am also cleared to 100% AVOID any hospital food at all so Mom will be on food duty! I will make and can a bunch of homemade, organic bone broth, and have a list of the other foods I'll be able to have while there like organic yogurt, eggs, and I also need to get some plain whey protein isolate to mix into my broth to keep up with protein needs for healing.

So, I am off to shop for bone broth as well as the magnesium citrate bottles for the cleanse. I will pull out the pressure canner and stock up for post-surgery. As an aside, if you ever plan to use a pressure canner and are choosing a stove, do NOT choose an induction glass top!! All canners are aluminum and will not work with induction without a conductor plate that make the whole process take FOREVER. I need to get a cadco electric countertop burner, but there is no time now. Also, at some point you WILL break the glass too while canning...fingers crossed that does not happen today!

Unplugging and Food

I finally made the decision to unplug from work a bit before my surgery. After my pre-op visits the gravity of this whole thing really hit me. I will finish up a few last things and go in for a few more hours, but mostly to say "see you May!" and such to some friends. Also, to be sure my plants have adequate water and love coverage while I am out.

Instead of working, I'll be trying to spend time with my family doing things I won't be able to do for a while. Like taking long walks down the road or through woods or going to the park to play. I will also be taking some time to just relax, meditate, and do some Reiki on myself to help get my cleared and ready for surgery and healing.

I will do some baking and meal prep with the kids and will bake Bear's birthday cake in advance! I did a quick organize and inventory of the main kitchen freezer and have done well stocking up on meals over the past 2 months. The current inventory includes:

- Chicken noodle soup
- Potato curry
- Chicken Curry
- Dal
- Saag Paneer
- Mushroom Risotto
- Cuban Black Beans and Rice
- Lamb Taco filling

- ➢ Butternut squash and pumpkin puree (which will be perfect to make into soup!)
- ➢ Chicken, Broccoli, Rice, and Cheese casserole
- ➢ Shredded rotisserie chicken (perfect to make enchiladas!)
- ➢ Banana muffins
- ➢ Peanut butter Banana muffin bars
- ➢ Plus, lots of chicken, pork, beef, and veggies

I am writing this as I am waiting for my canner to come up to pressure. I am canning a big batch of bone broth I made for my recovery when I am in the hospital. I'm making it in ½ pint jars so I don't waste any since I know I won't be able to have much at a time. I have also been waiting on the damned canner for hours because I have an induction cooktop that will not work with aluminum, which most canners are. It has to sit on a conductor plate and that really slows things down! Broth is going to be a big staple for me for the next few months. My gut is going to be so great come summer!

Speaking of food, it is a topic I'm fairly obsessed with right now. Probably because I have not been able to eat normally or really enjoy food for months. I am currently planning my hospital food, which will NOT be any hospital food. At all. It is in my chart...I am fully clear to have 100% outside food. Mom will be in charge based on my instructions before surgery. For the broth I will be sure she's got an electric kettle to heat it in...no sense ruining it in the microwave!

It is funny, once your system is cleared out (I get to do yet another bowel prep...oh joy), it's like a clean slate and I don't want to mess it up and I am focusing on only fueling with the best, homemade, organic goodness. Just feels wrong to immediately put hospital crap in it! Some of the foods I will begin with after the liquid diet part is past will be soft, low fiber things. Broth, eggs, yogurt, soft, cooked veggies, soft, cooked meats and fish. Once I start adding on to that diet, 4-6 weeks later, I will have to add each individual food one at a time. I still have a long way to go before I am eating fully normally. Months. I imagine I will drop a little more weight, though I've been doing pretty darn well holding down the weight loss on not many calories. For March I have averaged 1.75 lbs lost per week. My first goal will be to drop that to 1 lb or under per week. I really don't need to lose anymore and don't want to but am realistic that I still won't be getting loads of calories for a while.

Getting in Some Miles

One of the things I am acutely aware of, is that I am not going to be able to run for quite some time. Ironically, I absolutely hated running when I was younger! I have truly come to love it and I now cherish the time I get to spend running outside. It is almost meditative for me. I am also still super bummed that I will not be able to make it to Iron Man this year, but running was really the only discipline I had truly started training in.

I am officially off work now to spend as much time being active with my kids as possible before surgery. This afternoon I got to go on a 2-mile run with my three boys. It was the first time I took them running and they did fantastic! Especially Callister! Thatcher was about done a good half mile from home. Bear finished fine but was starting to get tired. He was also a fantastic pace buddy and ran right by my side, often holding my hand. I do believe Callister could have gone my normal 4 miles with me and done great! The kid had as much energy after 2 miles as he did when it started! I'll definitely do some one-on-one runs with just Callister!

Celebration

Hibachi is out go-to for family celebrations. Last night after Foo Foo arrived, we loaded up in the van and went to the Kani House. It was Elara's first time since she was young and watching her mesmerized face was just priceless! She was EXTREMELY impressed!! We had the birthday song with the drum for all 4 kids...it is "birthday season" after all!

I also figured since yesterday (Saturday) was my last day of eating allowed before my surgery, it should be delicious! I had a seared tuna with veggies - yum! I opted out of the regular hibachi due to the gluten. I am hopefully I'll be able to tolerate gluten again after I'm all healed from the surgery, but for now, it's just not worth the pain.

I also wanted to eat foods that will be restricted for the next 4-6 weeks as I heal and am on the "soft GI" diet. I filled up on broccoli, zucchini, onions, salad greens, nuts, and dried fruits! My post-surgery diet will be very boring. Mostly broth enhanced with whey isolate protein powder for protein, eggs, low fat yogurt, soft, cooked meats/fish, and soft, cooked and low fiber veggies (like carrots, yams, winter squash, green beans, etc.).

My post-surgery diet will need to be low fiber as I heal which will be hard for me since I love my veggies!! So, no raw veggies, high fiber things, nuts, seeds, dried fruits, or spicy, etc. BORING! But it will help my system heal so that is what I'll be doing. Once I am past the 4-6 weeks I'll get to start adding foods back. One at a time. So, it will be very slow going and probably take 6 months to get back to normal. The plus side is that I will know exactly how every single food affects me!

Today is Sunday and I am on the liquid diet ahead of surgery. I also just started a bowel prep, which means I got to drink a 10 oz bottle of magnesium citrate (black cherry flavored...not bad!). I had to drink it at 2 pm.

I got back from my final run at 1:46 pm. I like to push things sometimes, LOL! I have gotten in a bunch of great runs this past week. Highlights include 2 runs with the boys, including 1 where we dropped Thatcher and Bear off and Callister finished with me and completed his first 5K! Then yesterday I ran alone and had my best and fasted run yet! It felt amazing!

While I was up and running again about 3 weeks after my gallbladder surgery, I expect to be down longer this time. Not too long, but longer. There is more to heal from. This is going to sound super weird, but I plan to do "mental runs" (visualization) to help keep my progress going. I will let you know how that goes! (spoiler: I did not do this)

I am nearly packed for the hospital. I will shower right before bed and get up SUPER early to leave by 4:30 am and arrive by 5:30 am. Surgery is at 8:15 am.

I am asking that everyone please surround me in a pink healing blanket of love tomorrow morning. Just think about it and that will do it!

Change of Time

Got here a few minutes before 5:30 am, as directed. The check in lady notes "you're here early!" I am confused and note that I'm only 15 minutes early. Then she tells me my surgery is at 10 am. I say, no it is at 8:15. Sure enough my surgery got moved...and nobody bothered telling me!!

So, I walked the halls for a bit to get some extra steps in and am now curled up on a chair and ottoman trying to sleep a little. It is not going well.

Post-Whipple: Months 1-3

The Whipple & Hospital Stay

As with so many things in life, yesterday did not go exactly as planned, but all worked out in the end. The first thing that happened was minor. But annoying. My 8:15 am surgery got moved to 10 am and nobody ever called to tell me. We were at the hospital super early and I tried to catch a nap on some chairs.

I was finally taken back and got cleaned up with some special pre-surgical wipes and put on a gown, compression socks, and hospital socks. I got to rest under a heated air blanket which was awesome! They started 2 IVs and the epidural. The epidural was odd and for a bit I could not lift one of my legs.

I spoke with lots of people and a few folks from anesthesia. We discussed the healing statements I brought for them to read as I was being put under and waking up. I will post more on these later when I'm home and have my laptop.

I was in surgery about 8 hours. It turned out that both my ducts were tiny and difficult to open and the surgeon was not happy with his ability to get margins with just the ampullectomy. That meant that the update to my Mom was that they were converting to the full Whipple procedure. We knew this was a possibility and honestly, I would probably have needed it at some point anyway so better to do it now.

The Whipple procedure (pancreaticoduodenectomy), as a reminder, is a procedure to remove the head of the pancreas, the first part of the small intestine (duodenum), the gallbladder and the bile duct. The remaining organs are reattached to allow you to digest food normally after surgery

I am in recovery and will be here about a week, longer than planned due to the Whipple. They are taking great care of me and pain management is good. I am just exhausted!

Day 2: I Sat in a Recliner!

My first goal today was to take a walk. The PT came in super early. Maybe 6:30 am. I had been laying down all night and I managed to get to the sitting on the side of the bed. It fell apart from there. I got nauseated, started sweating, and had to lie back down. Probably from the epidural meds.

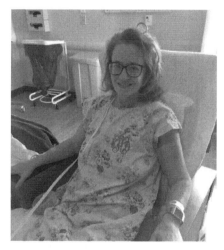

Later in the afternoon after having some broth, sitting up, and pain med with an anti-nausea med, I managed to get to a recliner, which was my second goal after walking (which I failed). I was able to sit up for an hour and 15 minutes. It was exhausting.

Tomorrow I hope to be able to walk...

I am also continuing with a breathing treatment protocol to help prevent pneumonia post anesthesia. Breathing is HARD after surgery and I had a breathing tube for a full 7 hours. I am supposed to do my breathing exercises hourly.

Day 4: A Pretty Bad Night

Yesterday got bad. I did not quite have the help that I needed to get back into bed on a few occasions after getting up to use the restroom. The result was that the line for my epidural got caught and pulled out a little bit. When it pulled out it basically stopped working. That was my continuous dose of pain medication. So, when it pulled out and stopped working I suddenly started to feel all of the pain.

This was around 3 o'clock or so in the afternoon and my pain went very quickly from zero to about a six. It went up from there and topped out at a full 10. We tried to work as quickly as we could with the pain management team. Everything happened in slow motion and took forever. I was finally able to get new meds to help get me over the hump. By that point when your pain is already at a 10 it becomes exceedingly difficult to control. We were able to get it down to about a six at that point I knew we needed to do better. It fluctuated between a six and a 10 for a good three hours.

They finally got approval, and everything put together to give me a pain pump that I would then need to control manually. The big benefit of the epidural was the continuous nature of it. The pain never really got below five last night. It was pretty excruciating, and I remember thinking I would rather just die right there and have to continue with that level of pain. Pretty bad.

I managed to get an amazing nurse in the morning and found this unacceptable and really pushed to pull the pain management team together quickly to come up with a solution that was more multi-faceted than a single pain pump. That coupled with meeting with my surgical team we were able to get in place some additional meds to help boost the pain pump. I still have the pump, but there are several other things as well.

It is all trial and error so one of the more error parts of the trial was the muscle relaxer that made me feel completely out of it. The pain part was controlled at this point, but I was so completely out of it. I still kind of am as the effects are not worn off yet. I am doing this whole post using talk to text on my phone which is difficult. Talking is difficult. Breathing has become difficult and starting last night I needed to be on a nasal cannula for oxygen. Without it my O2 stat was dropping into the mid-80s. I still cannot open my eyes and do this talking to text. I am just so tired.

Also, they increased the dose on my pain pump which is causing more nausea. Too much. So today has been fairly good for pain, pretty bad for nausea, and not awesome for breathing. This shit is hard! I am just rambling now and mostly trying to get all this down so that I can re-read it to know the timeline beyond just giving you all an update. I very much appreciate all the thoughts, prayers, well wishes, and food for my family!

Mom stayed a third night in the hospital with me last night and is at our house sleeping right now. I did not expect to be this high maintenance! Everything else is healing well though so despite being a difficult past 24 hours I am recovering well. There is no date on my release yet but expect it to be at least Monday or after.

Day 5: Another Rough Day

I was hoping to have all the pain and nausea and everything else under control today, but it did not come to pass. I have turned a small corner and I feel OK right now. Much of the day I was still in a lot of pain and having a lot of nausea. Just trying different combinations of meds. The worst was the muscle relaxer that I had for second time overnight. It does help with pain that makes me completely comatose.

Right now, my pain and nausea are fairly well under control they were hoping to be able to keep it this way. Speaking of IVs we thought my was leaking because it kept getting wet and we finally realized hours later after it had been removed and replaced, that it was the dressing on one of my drains. The good news on the drains that one has been removed already and we are hopeful the second one will come out tomorrow

Day 6, morning: Recovery is Hard and Slow

I am once again using talk to text with my eyes closed and not having the energy to re-read this, so please excuse all the typos and places it is confusing.

I honestly believed that by this time I would be feeling fairly good and that I would be going home today. I underestimated - this so hard. I think we finally figured out the right mix of meds to keep the pain manageable and to keep the nausea at bay. I had gotten into a terrible loop where the pain would cause nausea and I was not able to eat or drink which made me more nauseated which caused more pain. I have been fairly stable for about 24 hours now.

In the past 24 hours I have had both drains removed. One of them needed to stitches, which is done without an anesthetic. I have had my IV constant drip removed which gives me more mobility. I have been able to get up to go to the bathroom on my own and to take a few short walks down the hall.

I was able to get in my first significant meal yesterday and it was Campbell's tomato soup. At this point I'm not really caring what I eat just so long as it is something allowed, and I am also hungry for it. I have also had two chocolate pudding's and a few bites of vanilla since I have been here. But the big news is that today for lunch I transitioned to the soft G.I. diet which means I had real, actual food. My first meal was fish with a few carrots.

Mom has been great. I have had her sleeping here or with me 24 hours around the clock since I was admitted. I did not think I would need that kind of support, but I do. The meals people have provided have been tremendously helpful to them. I miss my kids. No visitors under 12 are allowed and I still do not think I look like what I want them to visit. The area of the hospital I am in is one level down from an ICU so I still get lots of extra attention from the staff which is good. I am by myself while Mom is resting. I am proud that I have been able to get up to use the restroom and have lunch on my own. But I did drop the call button once and had to walk on my own out to the hall to ask somebody to get it for me because I could not call in.

I am still not sure what the rest of recovery looks like. It really changes hour by hour. I have heard nurses say that some people will recover in the hospital for a Full 30 days after a Whipple. Apparently, this is one of the most complex surgeries anyone could have done. I am certain I will not be here that long, but it sunk in just how serious this is. I do not feel anywhere near ready to come home. And it sucks that I will not be home for Bear's birthday which is tomorrow. He will be six.

Day 6, evening: Still Struggling

Damnit. This shit is hard. The pain is intense. It has made me rethink future living will/advanced directive stuff. No extraordinary measures for me – I am not tough enough! If I ever have pain like again, say your goodbyes because I will be done.

Pain was better under control for a bit...then it came back. With a vengeance. Lots of confusion with orders. What was on a schedule versus available as needed. Came back after eating. I have been able to have real food today (grits, fish, carrots, green beans, yams, pork, pudding, etc.) but I am limited to 1/2 cup at a time and after liquids.

I have had two major pain experiences today. The first was just before dinner but I do not remember exactly when. I just know I got IV pain meds at 5 and that helped, but not for long.

The pain started getting bad after dinner and a surprise hiccup I think was also a contributor! I managed to get more IV pain meds at 9:10 pm...but it took over an hour to get the meds order straightened back out and into my system...with an 8-pain level. So bad! They had to page my surgeon, who was Celebrating his wife's birthday tonight.

Other fun odds and ends of the day include drain removal (ouch!!), a blood clot preventing shot in the stomach (every 24 hrs), 3 hallway walks, being given a med that doesn't work for me in place of one that does which delayed getting help into my system, a gown change, and a huge slice of mom guilt pie for not being home for Bear's 6th birthday tomorrow.

The help and support from family, friends, and work (my boss and his family took the kids all afternoon!) has been humbling and amazing and something I will be forever grateful for! I anticipated needing some meals. I had no idea we would need such basic help with watching the kids so that my mom could be here 24 hours a day for so many days.

I truly hope nobody I know, or anybody really, ever has to go through anything like this. Please, take care of yourselves proactively. Get all of the screenings. See your doctor. Listen to your body. Fill it with good foods and stay away from chemicals. Nothing is more important than your health!

Day 7: Same Status, Different Day

I keep hoping I will have some groundbreaking status update to give you. To say I have turned a corner or am feeling significantly better and stronger. I am not. My pain is under better control than it has been, but I still need "the big guns" several times per day. I go from a 2/3 on the pain scale to a 4/5 incredibly fast. 5 is my 'tipping point' where I know if we don't catch it and treat quickly, it'll tip over to an 8+ at lightning speed and take many, many hours to recover from.

I wanted to add that I am still grateful that I am recovering well, all things considered. It is the little things right now that that are keeping me going. The extra responsive nurse. The thoughtful food services person who brings me 'extra' of something even though I can only tolerate a few nibbles anyway. The IV nurse who added this little flower and 'Madonna glove' to make my IV more comfortable.

Day 7: 48 Hours?

Still need to work on dialing in some routines, but I am getting there. Slowly but surely, emphasis on the slowly. The surgeon let me know that I've passed all the major risk zones so that's great! The hope is that I might get to go home around Tuesday.

Dinner was about 4 teeny bites plus a few bites of cottage cheese...but it was good! Also, I have basically moved in at this point!

Day 8: Home Tomorrow!

Presuming everything continues to go according to plan, I will get to be coming home tomorrow! As you know this has been an incredibly difficult week and I have struggled mightily with pain.

The final piece of this puzzle that will allow me to go home will be a switch from an IV medication for pain to the oral version. I have had my first dose of the oral med at 9:30 AM and at noon it is still working well so I am very hopeful! I will be on a schedule with the pain med on top of alternating Tylenol and Motrin. We decided on the schedule because I would wait too long and try to push through the pain and would reach the tipping point before asking for meds which made it much harder to control.

I did have a pretty shitty night last night though. At 2:40 in the morning I asked for my pain med, as prescribed by my surgeon, and got both yelled at and lectured by a nurse for a solid 20 minutes about how I should not be using this pain med anymore. She argued with me that I could not possibly be feeling the pain I was feeling. She very strongly implied that I wanted to extend my stay in the hospital to avoid going home as well as strongly implied that I may be abusing the pain med.

That being said, I have used much less of the pain medication then was even prescribed, and less frequently than allowed. I had also only been on it for two days and it was the first and only thing that was working to control incredibly severe pain. It is also the medication suggested by the pain management team and my surgeon. It was

71

shocking and incredibly upsetting and I damn near checked myself out AMA and drove my self-home last night.

She was immediately pulled off my service and has been dealt with. We are back on track with controlling the pain which should help me go home. When the pain was uncontrolled, I was unable to eat, as well as was still having a hard time drinking due to the thrush. Uncontrolled pain also makes it harder to do the thing that helps with recovery the most, which is moving around and walking. I am still completely stunned that even happened.

I am back on track, doing well, excited to get home, and finally able to eat and drink well. My lunch was some of the sous vide egg bites from Starbucks and a piece of gluten-free toast. It was oddly amazing!

Day 1 at home!

After 8 VERY long days in the hospital, I'm so happy to be home and back in my own bed!!! In my pink flamingo sheets!

Why a theme? Just because! Flamingos are pink, feathery, whimsical, kitschy, and make me happy! I am trying to inject as much fun into this decidedly UNfun process as possible.

Despite not being able to shower yet I am finally in fresh, clean clothes! A pink flamingo nightshirt over a light compression tank top (feels better like my insides are held together better), with leggings and pink flamingo socks. The view is better too – I really adore my bedroom! Though it doesn't usually have a giant TV, this seemed like the right time to indulge in a little TV from bed.

So now, I rest. And sleep. A LOT. I only finally got true sleep for the first time in 8 days starting last night. The rest of my 'sleep' has been extremely light and mostly drug induced. Also, in the hospital you're CONSTANTLY being checked on and poked and prodded and checked.

The worst was this morning at 5 am. I could have slept until 5:30 when my next meds were due which is what made it extra frustrating. A woman comes bounding in with the scale exclaiming "it's time to get your weight!" Let me also add the context that the room was completely dark, and I was SOUND asleep. Also, the bed I was in has a control panel that she could have used to press a few buttons to get my weight. I told her to come back when I was up.

I don't exactly bound out of bed these days. Getting up still involves a hearty assist from an electronic bed. Super easy at the hospital! For home I bought a mattress genie (from bed bath and beyond...with the 20% off coupon, of course!) and it is basically an inflatable bed wedge that you operate with a remote – cool!

Mom just got me all unpacked and is making me a dinner snack – an egg with some cottage cheese. Great protein and a welcome change from the hospitals lovely powdered 'eggs.'

So, my diet now. I'm on a soft GI diet and need to eat very small amounts every 2-3 hrs. High protein, low fiber, soft, cooked everything, low fat, low sugar, and no spices yet. I also need to take pancreatic enzymes before I eat anything. Without them, my body will not be able to absorb the nutrients and I'm at risk for malabsorption and malnutrition from it.

One thing I did not realize about the Whipple, is that part of my stomach was removed as part of the reconstruction process. It is smaller. Like a gastric bypass maybe? I cannot eat more than 1/2 cup at a time. I will probably continue (not on purpose!) to lose some weight as my body figures out how to digest and process food. I am down to 144 lbs. Not too bad, but even I see how thin I am now. (spoiler alert: I ultimately drop to an alarming 117 lbs as my lowest)

Becoming a Whipple Warrior

Ok, eggs are ready and it's time for meds!

Day 4 at Home

I am getting so much better! While I am still on alternating Tylenol and Motrin around the clock, I haven't had a 'big' pain pill in over 13 hours!! I had been on them ever 4 hrs around the clock. This is HUGE progress!!

My only minor setback was dinner last night. I wanted to be normal and eat with the family and we had Asian takeout. I was careful with ordering but forgot about soy sauce containing gluten so now I am dealing with the multi day aftermath of a gluten attack. I am bloated (about 2 lbs worth) and feel very full, but it is not as bad as it could be. It was not a crazy amount of gluten, but it was enough. The next few days will see me drinking extra water and having mostly just yogurt, Turkey, green beans, and blueberries. Safe, single ingredient things.

I have been spending most of my time in bed with some time in my chair in my room too. I take frequent walks around the house and have taken a few showers (so good!). The boys have each spent some nice one on one time with me in the bed watching TV and talking. They like to get "rides" when I pump the bed up and down!

My incision is healing incredibly well! It goes from right under my breasts vertically straight down and around my belly button. It is basically my entire stomach! It was just closed with surgical glue...a LOT of glue! Plus two small side holes where the drains were. One had stitches and one did not. The one with stitches feels totally unnecessary and I want to have my mom take them out. So unnecessary! She is a nurse, and we have the proper

suture scissors. We did not end up having her remove
them.

Months 1-2

A few days after my last blog post, the same day as Bear's amazing birthday party that my fantastic friends threw for him, I spiked a 103 fever with extraordinary pain and was taken to the ER via ambulance. Ride #2. I was taken to the ER near me, not where I had my surgery. They admitted me and despite lots of IV drugs they were unable to control my pain. I was immobile in the bed for 2 full days with pain that fluctuated between and 8-10. I wanted to die. Truly. It was that bad.

CAT scan showed some fluid buildup around my pancreas but nothing super alarming. Since this hospital is not full of whipple experts, I got an ambulance transfer down to "my" hospital, so I'd be under the care of my surgeon. Thank goodness the pain management team was right there when I arrived, and I was quickly set up with a self-controlled pain pump full of Dilaudid (4x stronger than morphine). Within hours I could breathe again, and the pain was down to a bearable 5-6, even as low as a 4 sometimes. For perspective, I rank natural childbirth as a 4.

The pain and fever were coming from an infection, so I got loaded with antibiotics and now I have an Infectious Disease doc on the team. My left lung was also dangerously near collapse, so I had a lot of breathing treatments. When my pain goes through the roof, I literally cannot breathe. My breathing was super slow and shallow. Misery. Total misery!

Since I was still in loads of pain I was not moving or walking like I needed to. I physically could not. The 7 days I was in the hospital this time nearly broke me. I did not think I'd ever recover and get my life back. I was completely unable to put my positive face on. I could feel depression settling over me.

By the time I was released I was both mentally and emotionally broken/spent, as well as physically deformed. A combination of a constant IV drip plus not moving with the head of the leg and foot of the bed slightly raised left nearly 30 extra pounds of fluid that settled from mid-thigh and up my stomach. My stomach was bloated/distended by a full 10 inches. It was incredibly painful!

It took 2 weeks before any of that fluid weight began to come off. The pills they gave me for it did not work. Finally, fennel seeds soaked in water overnight started moving it. Once it started coming off, I lost 14 of those pounds over 3 days! I knew I had been losing "real" weight as well but with all the fluid weight I had no idea how much. I know that at that point I had lost 2 inches off each arm and 3 inches off each thigh.

As I recovered from the infection and lost the fluid weight, I hit another stumble. I started having a pain in my abdomen again. It started the day after I saw my surgeon for a follow up and was told I was "on the right track" and did not have to come back for a full month!

The pain got worse over the next 4-5 days. I was hoping it was gas/fluid shifting around. Then I got a low temp a little over 99. Due to the lower right quadrant location, I worried maybe it was my appendix. Thinking, well shit, that is about that last organ than can even come out without killing me!

I finally realized I should have it checked out so drive myself to the ER near me. All the while thinking surely, they'll tell me it's just gas and send me home. I took the van so was really hoping I was just being silly!

I got there and realized that the only nice thing about arriving via ambulance is that you go directly back to a room! I did not mind the wait...it meant I wasn't the most serious thing there. The wait was 1 hr 25 min.

The nurse was sure it was appendicitis. CAT scan showed not appendicitis but 2 abdominal abscesses! 1 was 8 cm (fairly large!) and the other only 2 cm. They called my surgeon to consult and determine if they could drain it there or not. He wanted me transferred down and admitted me personally. So, another ambulance transfer for me! That one was expensive too since it was considered "elective." Except that it was not.

I spent the night, until a little before 4 am, in the ER waiting on transfer paperwork. They had to shuffle things to find me a room. The next day I was able to get the abscess drained, which terrified me! The drug 'cocktail' was AMAZINGLY effective at making me not notice or care which was great! I had a JP drain placed and I will spare you the details other than saying it was a damned good thing it was drained and not left in there! While I was in this time, I flat out refused any IV fluids or pain meds. I did not want a repeat of the fluid gain from the last hospital stay!!I was able to go home the next day, with the drain still in. The following day I returned to the surgeon where they removed the drain.

The next day...I went to a party! It was my first non-medical outing and though all I did was ride in a car then sit on a sofa, it was great! I am still slow and recovering, but it was after the drain was removed that I feel like a corner had truly been turned!

8 Weeks Status

Thought I would give a whipple recovery update as I am exactly 8 weeks out from my surgery. The most helpful thing recently has been a FB group I found for "whipple warriors" who have survived this surgery...so much great information, community, and support. If you are also a Whipple Warrior search for the group: Whipple Surgery Survivor Group. I have learned so much! Especially since this was not the surgery I had planned and prepared for.

Had I realized just what a big deal this surgery is and that I will be dealing with challenges from it for the rest of my life, not sure what decision I would have made. Since most people who are "whipped" have the surgery for pancreatic cancer (and are lucky to even have the whipple as an option!) I feel extra grateful that mine was not for cancer. Pancreatic cancer is one of the most deadly with only 9% surviving by year 5 post diagnosis.

I am still working through issues with abdominal pain, but nowhere near as bad or as frequent as earlier so good progress. Some days are better than other. It hurts most when changing position (laying to sitting, sitting to standing, etc.). It hurts if I get too hungry or If I have 1 single bite too much. I am working hard on rebuilding my stamina and have done 2 errands in the car and am taking a lot more walks. I can finally do stairs again too. I also washed and dried Elara's hair by myself! It is really the

little things at this point

Naturally, since it is still me, I did too much Saturday and have been recovering the past 2 days. I am working on pacing myself but am hyper aware that I will be heading back to work soon (yay!) and need to be able to drive 37 miles (each way!) plus be productive when I'm there!

I am still working on what I can eat, how much, and when, along with the best dosing of the pancreatic enzymes I take to help with digestion. I am down 12 lbs. since surgery and trying hard to not lose anymore! My target is to eat 8x/day. Those 12 lbs. came with 2.5 inches lost off each arm and a full 4 inches lost off each thigh! During the second hospital stay I actually gained 29 lbs of fluid from the IV (all in my stomach which gained a full 10" of bloat!!) so in the 8 weeks since surgery I've gained and lost a lot and it's been physically painful!

I have lost a lot of muscle and will need to focus on rebuilding it! My bum is so flat and wasted away that I had to get a special gel pad to be able to sit in chairs without significant pain from sitting right on bone. Oh, and the loose skin, especially my legs, is worse than ever! I am now down a total of 181 lbs. It is too much.

I still get really, really exhausted. More exhausted than pregnancy even. It will hit out of nowhere and there is no other option than a nap. This worries me about returning to work! I am at least sleeping ok at night at this point. I can also sleep on my sides now but cannot change position unless I'm awake. It takes focus and effort.

I am mostly staying positive, but it is hard. I miss my life pre-surgery. I miss not even thinking about my belly. Hell, I miss having a gallbladder, bile duct, pyloric valve, all of my stomach, the head of my pancreas, duodenum, and a good chunk of my small intestines! I know how lucky I am that we found my ampullory adenoma BEFORE it silently turned into a killer cancer. This recovery is just really, really hard. From what I understand, most people take a fully year to fully recover...and even then, there are issues that just last forever.

9 Week Status

I am now 9 weeks out from the biggest surgery I'll ever have and I'm happy to say I'm doing pretty well! I am driving now and it feels pretty normal. I can do small errands and am now finally up and dressed most of the day! I have even made the bed a few times (ok just twice, but it's a start!). I have made a few meals, packed some lunches for the boys for camp, and am with Elara solo all week while the boys are at camp! I could not have done this even last week.

I am still working on the eating and digesting thing but it is getting better. I can pretty much eat what I want, just in much smaller portions, which is fine. Sometimes I cannot even finish a whole string cheese, but sometimes I can have a whole taco. Depends on the day and how I am feeling.

The eating part is still easier than actually absorbing the nutrients from the food and digesting properly. I am still losing weight and am now sitting at 132 lbs which is 15 lbs down from my surgery day. Pretty much everyone who has been "whipped" loses weight after surgery, so this is totally normal and expected. I am also lucky to still be in a healthy weight range even with the continued loss.

My next appointment will include blood work to see if I am absorbing enough nutrients (I think I probably am). This will be a lifelong thing now. The plus side here is that I do not really have to worry about regaining all the weight I lost!

As for pain, it is still there but improving. I still have not had one single second without pain though. I was not even this aware of my abdomen when I was pregnant! I can finally roll over in bed now without fully waking up and wincing in pain and moving very slowly so that is a big deal! Getting up and down from chairs is getting easier but I still love slow and the longer I sit the harder it is to get up. My scar is looking great though!

My newest pain though is my back! I have been laying and sitting with my back supported for so long that my back muscles are out of practice!! Even just sitting up in a chair and not leaning on the back is hard work. My entire back is sore all the time, so I am laying on a heating of a lot!

I go back to work in 2 weeks and have been working on rebuilding my stamina. I've been to some get togethers and play dates and even my first girls' night since surgery! I do still need to nap which is what is worrying me the most about going back to work. It hit a point where the exhaustion/fatigue is absolutely overwhelming and intense and there is literally nothing to do but sleep. It happens most days and not even from overdoing it. It is just a thing now. It even puts pregnancy exhaustion to absolute shame! And I am NOT a napper so it's been quite humbling.

I am still restricted physically and cannot life more than 10 lbs. Due to the large vertical incision I am at decent risk for a hernia and I want to do everything possible to avoid that!! The incision itself is healing super well. I lifted a box of frozen burgers last week and immediately felt pain in my stomach, so I am being extra careful now!

While 10 lbs is the max even a gallon of milk is hard for me right now Did you know that a gallon of milk weighs 8 lbs when full? I am going to ask my surgeon for a PT recommendation when I go back next week. I want to know what movements and exercises are ok and what is not. I know I'll need to strengthen my abs but need to know how to do that without risking a hernia. I am just focusing on walking for now which I know is not only safe, but very beneficial in my recovery.

Another interesting thing is that I appear to be tolerating gluten now! I learned something fascinating from a woman from my "whipple warriors" group who has celiac. When hers was tested it started in her duodenum and since that plus part of the small intestines is removed during a whipple, she can have gluten now! So, it makes sense why I'm ok with in now too. So interesting! Still not going to test this out with a plate of pasta, but I have had small bites of gluten here and there and been ok! If I just do not have to worry about cross contamination or trainings with small amounts of gluten (like soy sauce) that's a massive win!! (spoiler alert: I now, 18 month out have no issues with gluten! Even a plate of pasta)

Speaking of gluten, I'm signing off to make some lemon blueberry cupcakes with a Elara!

My 1st Whipple Attack

Thank goodness I knew about these from my amazing Whipple Warrior group otherwise I straight up would have panicked! Some people have them, some do not. They can happen often or once in a lifetime. I had 4 last night!

No idea what caused it. Different things bring them on for different people. For me it felt like an actual knife was stabbed directly into my pancreas and twisted around. I also felt an incredibly intense squeezing spawning feeling in my upper abdomen just at and below my ribs. It basically felt like being in a knife fight while in the most intense part of childbirth! I could not speak. I was unable to move (was thankfully in the recliner or I would have just dropped to the floor!). All I could do was the blowing out kind of breathing I did during labor. The pain was at a solid 8. I got hot, flushed, and started to sweat. I did not check but I am certain my pulse and blood pressure also shot up too. Mercifully, it only lasted 2-3 minutes. The next three were ever so slightly less intense and were shorter.

I really hope I am not prone to these. They are completely debilitating, and I spent the rest of the night with a heating pad on low over my abdomen in bed. It was exhausting! I am trying to figure out if there was a trigger. From what I've gathered from my group it can be anything from certain foods, too much food, digestives issues, or bending/moving too much (i.e. generally overdoing it). I also learned not to eat/drink anything after it that could be irritating, or it could get worse.

One of the worst parts of my attack was that it happened with 10 min left on my chicken biryani!! While I refrained from having a full meal I did try a few bites, even knowing it could make the attacks worse. I HAD to try it and it was DELICIOUS!! Though I suspect I may have avoided the next 3 attacks had I not added any food into my system. And I do think it was just food, not the biryani specifically. I did also make sure to set aside a container of leftovers that I told the family not to touch so I can have it today.

As an aside: that I am both wanting to cook and cooking again is a HUGE leap forward in recovery for me! I even made my first trip to our local Indian grocery yesterday for supplies and a new spice box. For me, cooking is a huge passion and I just do not feel like myself unless I am cooking. I am thrilled to be up to cooking again. Though I needed help to lift the cast iron Dutch oven to the stove because it is still too heavy for me. I may still need some help, but I am getting there!

If you are ever around me when I have a Whipple attack, you will for sure know it!! When it is happening please just give me some space and do NOT try to ask me any questions. I will not be able to answer you and it will be distracting and frustrating. I just need to breathe through it.

After, I will probably need to rest quietly for a while and hope it is an isolated attack. Another reason I will need a quiet spot to rest in so I am in a comfortable spot in case I have more attacks. But mostly know that it is not dangerous, I do not need to go to the hospital, and it will pass.

This is just another part of my new normal. Hopefully, this will be the first and only time it happens, but I'd rather be prepared and have those around me be prepared as well. I had one on one talks with all the kids about it so they are not scared when it happens. Most of the kids barely noticed this one because Bear and Callister were wrestling and fighting – boys! Elara was busy watching a show. Thatcher was the most aware.

11 Week Status & Back at Work

Exactly 11 weeks post-Whipple I went back to work. On one hand this seems like a super long time to be out recovering. On the other hand, many take so much longer recovering and either go back 9-12 months later or flat out retire. I am definitely one of the lucky ones in that my recovery has been *relatively* quick and uneventful (even including 2 subsequent hospital stays!).

From a stamina perspective, last week I still was not sure I'd be able to come back this week. Progress is still slow and there are many things I can do one week that the prior week I could not fathom. This is the first week I have not taken a nap almost daily. As a tradeoff, there have been several evenings that saw me in bed by 5 pm! My stamina has improved a lot this week and Wednesday was a good day. My stomach on the other hand, is still all over the place and I suspect will remain my biggest challenge.

It has been wonderful to reconnect with my work family. And my friends at work really are like family and I am so grateful to get to say this. I realized early in the week that catching up after 11 weeks is VERY different from catching up after, say, 2 weeks. I was able to basically start over which was very freeing! No emails from 11 weeks ago are still relevant so most of it was filed away so I can search for specific things if needed, but meant I did not need to sift through thousands of emails!

As for how I felt pain wise, that is still an issue. I had splurged a bit on Sunday by having 2 mini cupcakes and part of a cookie. I thought maybe I would be ok, but I was not. While fats and sugars are the things most likely to throw me into distress, it is really the processed sugars that kill me. Thankfully, they are not a part of my regular diet and I am not even particularly fond of them. Sugars are only an occasional splurge item, but apparently one I can ill afford now, or maybe ever.

It threw my stomach into the hellacious spasms and the digestive distress that has become my new normal. I was not able to eat any solid food again until Thursday (I can still get in calories via liquid diet). There were a few times I had to pull my car over during my commute to let waves of pain work themselves out. Kind of a scary experience to experience such blinding pain while driving!!

There is a 19 lb difference between when I left work and when I came back. It was quite noticeable!

The not being able to eat consistently and only able to eat small amounts when I can (remember, part of my stomach was removed so I cannot physically consume more) certainly contributes to the stamina issue...as well as the continued inability to stabilize my weight. Thankfully, I am still at a healthy weight for my height of 5' 6" and while still trending down overall, it's slowed significantly over the past 2 weeks and I'm hovering around the 128 mark +/- 3 or so lbs. I'm hoping to at least not go any lower but am realistic that I'll still probably drop a bit more as I continue to fine tune my enzymes and diet in terms of how much and how often. I am already in sizes 2-4 in pants (so surreal!!) and XS/S in tops so will soon run out of clothing sizes if I can't get my weight settled in!

We went on a walk and I made it just over 1 mile – my longest since surgery! I desperately need to put on some muscle!! Most of the post-Whipple weight loss feel like it has been muscle loss. I just feel weak. I am also still limited to 10 lbs of lifting, which is basically a gallon of milk. I am not allowed to do ANY abdominal exercises for a minimum of 6 months (so another 3 months from here) due to the risk of a hernia along my massive vertical incision.

I am, however, allowed to walk and swim and I'm now up to just over a mile of walking which is awesome! The goal is that any weight I am finally able to add on will be muscle. From my online "Whipple Warrior" group, it seems like for a lot of us weight beings to stabilize sometime after 6 months or so. I am hoping it happens a bit sooner, but it gives me hope that this will not be a permanent issue in any case. It will, however, be likely that gaining weight will always be a challenge due to how I now digest and process food and nutrients, coupled with the Whipple diet and portion sizes. So that is good news since statistically, so many people who lose weight go on to regain it! I also think that since I lost the weight by fundamentally changing my food lifestyle and not by any diet or fad, that I will be ok there.

The last update I'll share is from my last visit with my surgeon which was last Friday. I am doing well and will not need to go back until December! At that point I will have a new MRI for a post-Whipple baseline. From there I will see my surgeon once per year and will get an endoscopy and colonoscopy every 5 years (unless my genetic results dictate otherwise...those results come July 11).

I also called the medical practice he works with a lot to

find a primary care physician since I now need a "team." I do not want to be a doctor's first or only Whipple patient, so I spoke with a nurse there and she is going to speak with all the doctors and see who the best fit for me will be based on my history. I am now an "interesting case" both due to my Whipple, as well as because I had it for an ampullory adenoma which is extraordinarily rare. Good times!

3 Months Status

Finally! I am finally starting to feel much more like my old self. I am still struggling (often, mightily!) with what I can, and more importantly, cannot eat, but my weight is more or less stable now which is pretty major. I know for certain that extra sugar (in sweet treats...fruits are fine), more specifically processed sugar, destroys me for DAYS. Horrible cramping and pain and a lot of time spent in the bathroom. Extra fats do the same thing, but I can tolerate a bit more of that than of sugar.

I have come to accept now that even the 'treats' just are not worth it. It is not a healthy cycle to be eating what I want, paying for it for the whole next week, then starting that over. So, I have resigned myself to slow and steady and really and truly adding things one at a time and logging all food and the, ahem, consequences.

For someone who loves intricate flavors, lots of seasoning, and spicy things, this is HARD! But I'm going to do it and the family is doing it with me. This means more chicken and fish over beef and pork, and 'boring' veggies that are lightly steamed or roasted (in MCT oil since I can digest MCTs without pancreatic enzymes!). Less spices for now, and while the rest of the family probably will not, I am laying off dairy for a bit. Not super far off my normal diet, just blander for the time being so I can pinpoint my triggers.

Food aside, I am SUPER excited that my stamina is coming back!! I am walking more (up to 2.5 miles!) and faster (18:25 min/mi), and more often. I even went on a little hike last night which I did not think I'd be able to do again! My brain finally feels like it is unfogging a bit more at work and things are coming into focus again.

That is something that really surprised me when I can back

– my inability to focus and digest information! So incredibly frustrating!! I am still slower and less focused that pre-surgery, but I'm getting there. Sometimes the wrong words still come out though...like when I tried to tell Winslow (yes, I talk to my dog...do not pretend like you don't either - ha!) "I need to take the brownies out of the oven" and it came out as "I need to get the brown browns out of the office." Yeah, weird!

We had a great party for Callister's VERY belated 7th birthday and an awesome 4th of July a few days later. Lots of swimming and grilling and friends! I learned that as I much as I LOVE pulled pork, it does not love me in equal measure. Same with baked beans, potato salad, and coleslaw...though in fairness I am not sure which of those foods are triggers for me (see above!). Callister is becoming a regular fish in the pool and can now touch the bottom of the deep end which he is super psyched about!

On the 4th we had some good friends over for swimming, eating, and general catching up – so fun! Later that evening we had s'mores and shot off an obscene number of massive fireworks from the driveway – country living at its finest! Overall, I'm learning to relax more, not sweat the small stuff, and just enjoy this lovely life! I have also been doing a fair amount of floating around in the pool not worrying about a thing.

Post-Whipple – Months 4-6

Clean Genes!! Cancer genetic test results...

I have AMAZING news!!! I got the results from my genetic testing for a variety of testing back today. I asked them to test for "everything" because KNOWLEDGE IS POWER and they tested 67 genes...a massive testing panel!!! The tests include the genes for breast, pancreatic, colon, ovarian, brain, and a number of others.

****ALL 67 CAME BACK NEGATIVE...NORMAL...NO GENETIC PREDISPOSITIONS TO ANY CANCERS ****

My testing was through the Northside Hospital Cancer Institute, through my surgeon.

Farewell Sugar – Dumping Syndrome, you suck!

I have known for well over a month that I simply cannot tolerate sugar anymore. Fruits are ok, but I stick to lower sugar options like berries and red grapes. I think I have mentioned that processed sugars "destroy me" so I thought I'd explain a bit and give an example of just how sensitive I am to it now and what happens when I have it.

One of the delightful new things I am prone to post-Whipple is the accurately named "dumping syndrome." Certain foods make this more likely and will cause a rapid absorption of water from the body, thus 'dumping' said food very quickly into the intestines and rapidly out the other end. And I do mean RAPIDLY! Sugars do this to me every time!! Also, if I eat too much at a single sitting. Also, randomly, which is oh so fun.

The only "nice" thing about it is that whenever I experience constipation (which can be VERY painful post-Whipple), all it takes to solve the problem is for me to have a Reese's peanut butter cup or two! Much more effective than Dulcolax, MiraLAX, or other similar drugs...and delicious! Silver linings and all!

Dumping syndrome is also part of why I try to eat small amounts and very often. My doctor has me aiming to eat EIGHT times per day (I am still losing weight!). Obviously, that needs to be small portions because it means I'm eating every hour and a half or so...and frankly, I'm just not hungry enough so soon after eating to do this all the time. I basically need to have a trickle of food working through me most of the time. Eating too much can cause dumping, or pain, cramping, bloating, etc. Even a single bite beyond what I should have can put me into a world of hurt!

How do I know I am about to experience dumping? Usually

within 10-15 minutes I will get hot, flushed, shaky, and nauseated. I will need to lie down. Then I will be running to the bathroom! Thankfully, it goes quick and is typically over in about 45 minutes to the point I feel pretty good again.

This happened to me this morning. The whole episode was over quickly, but the trigger demonstrated just now sensitive I am to sugar. I have a few supplements/vitamins I take daily. A few are in gummy form (because I just hate swallowing so many pills!) and some are capsules. Things like a multivitamin, biotin, COQ10, calcium chews, turmeric, grapeseed extract, vitamin C, and probiotics. I added a new gummy today. Vitamin B12. I noticed the gummies had a sugar coating, in addition to whatever sugars are used to make the gummy and kind of gave it the side eye. Sure enough, that small amount of extra sugar tipped me over my limit and immediately out it all came!! So, I've now finally resigned myself to simply avoid all sugars.

And the worst part? While I never had a sweet tooth before, post-Whipple, I totally do! Down the road I may rest test sugar with SMALL bites of dark chocolate (my favorite!!) and see what my limit is so I know in case I want a small treat here and there.

Post-Whipple Diet – Doing it Right

I messed up. I did not at first, but over the past few weeks, I totally blew it. I knew shortly after my Whipple that my diet needed to be adjusted slightly. I was already eating healthy, but I had fuller meals and occasional treats. I was too eager to hop right back where I left off once the worst of the acute healing phase had passed. My surgeon wanted me eating "everything" and often! So, when I was feeling mostly better I did just that!

Then I had my first whipple attack and have been struggling to recover and get my eating back on track ever since. I knew I needed to fast for a bit and get started eating again after slowly and careful after that attack. While I did the fasting part, I was so hungry by the time I was ready for food, I'd overdo it. Then feel rotten again, then try to fast a day or two and start again...and so on and so forth. Horrible, terrible, no go, unhealthy pattern!! Not anything I am proud to admit and frankly, it's taken a lot of time for me to admit this publicly because I feel pretty dumb about it.

I think that while eating healthy is generally easy for me, and I mostly only want healthy foods anyway, there is something very different about NEEDING to eat a certain way versus just WANTING to. The stakes are higher. Pre-Whipple (and pre-issues that led me to getting the Whipple), if I splurged too much, I'd just get right back on track and all was well. Now, if I eat too much (by even one single bite!) or have the wrong food (like sugars or fatty/greasy things like pulled pork), I am in some serious pain. Beyond that, if I trigger a pancreatitis episode (last one landed me int he hospital in agonizing pain for SEVEN days), that in and of itself can be fatal. With pancreatitis, your pancreas basically begins to digest itself.

So, after having too much pulled pork BBQ (my favorite!!), potato salad, coleslaw, baked beans, a tiny bit of mac n cheese, plus some brownies, I was in a world on pain! Bloating, inflammation, cramping, you name it! I didn't actually have crazy super-sized portions or anything, but it was clearly 'enough' to trigger pain. Fearing another Whipple Attack or pancreatitis I decided it was time to really buckle down and get my diet back on track. Properly and for the long term.

I have been liquid fasting (still getting some calories, nutrition, and supplements so I'm ok!), and today started back with a pancreas soothing green juice made from kale, spinach, parsley, cilantro, ginger, lemon, and green apple. This will help my gut start waking up again and will 'test' my tolerance for those foods. My goal is to build back slowly, adding foods 1 or 2 at a time (past this initial green juice and smoothie phase!) and taking careful notes of any symptoms I experience. I will then place each food on my "safe" or "restricted" list. I have a spreadsheet that goes out until early September! This will help me stay on track to plan and know what foods I add which days (adding new things every 1-2 days), as well as show me an up-to-date list of 'safe' foods I can make recipes from!

I am starting with veggies and no fats to be easy on my system. After the green juice, I'll move onto broth, soft, cooked veggies, then start adding in grains like rice, quinoa, barley, and oats. Then some lower sugar fruits like berries and red grapes. I will also work in lentils, beans, and chickpeas. Once I am good there, I move onto animal proteins starting with egg whites, then chicken, fish, turkey. I'll also test low fat cheese, like string cheese, and other low-fat dairy like yogurt and cottage cheese. Nuts like almonds, cashews, and pistachios will be on my list as well, after starting fats with MCT oil/coconut oil.

I tried to front load my 're-entry" diet with items that will start getting me both excellent nutrition, as well as more calories and protein (i.e. lentils with veggies, egg white omelets, rice and veggies, etc.). I think it is a solid plan and will help me get into a good pattern of eating 6-8 times per day with foods I both tolerate well and that have the low fat and high protein I need to be healthy. My foods will be bland until I have a solid base built, then I'll start adding my spices again!

This is me truly accepting my 'new normal' (and I hate that term!) and trying to relearn what healthy is for me going forward. I want to be sure I am putting excellent and usable fuel into my body so I can keep a healthy function for my pancreas, liver, and the rest of my remaining organs! I also want to teach my children how important it is to feed your body with goodness. I think one of my biggest challenges will be eating both enough and often enough. I am confident I'll get there though!

Diet Struggles Continue

Best laid plans. Right?

I was so confident in my plan to reintroduce foods and get my diet squared away. I just knew I was doing things right and was excited to get several foods onto my safe list. I had done a lot of research on the best post-pancreatitis foods since I'm coming off not pancreatitis, but a bad pancreas flare, and one of my sources said to start with green juice (spinach, kale, cilantro, parsley, dandelion (didn't have this), green apple, ginger, and green apple) to get nutrients back in gently.

Made logical sense to me...also I *wanted* green juice. That meant I was willing to completely ignore the fact that I needed a post-WHIPPLE diet and not a post-pancreatitis diet. It is different. I am still working on accepting my new reality and trying to grant myself a bit of grace as I do.

A post-Whipple diet is bland and beige. It is broth, rice, plain chicken, and fish. It is toast, applesauce, crackers, and mashed potatoes. I, however, always crave and want brightly colored fresh veggies and fruits...which can be terrible to the freshly whipped system! Leafy green especially tends to be extremely difficult for many of us Whipplers. Again, I am still working on accepting that I have much different needs and tolerances now. I will get there.

Here is what happened last night. I happily got my Champion Juicer all set up readied my organic ingredients. I made my juice and double strained it. I wanted to be sure to remove any of the fibers, so I was getting straight juice to be easy on my fasted system. I took a teeny sip and realized I needed to dilute it so added an equal part of water so it was only half juice and half water.

It made a pretty big 8-10 oz glass and I sipped on half of it thinking I should start slow and make sure it was fine then have the other half this morning. Pretty quickly my back started hurting and my tummy got very noisy. As the evening went on, the pain got worse and worse. I was also super gassy with bubbles that were 'popping' very painfully in my belly. It was 100% a terribly angry pancreas with abdominal pain that was radiating very intensely to my back. I tent to feel my pancreas pain most intensely in my back...and have for years (just did not know what it was!). Pain peaked somewhere around a 5. For reference, I put natural childbirth at a 4.

That was from 4-5 ounces of 100% diluted juice!! I know without a doubt that had I drank the entire glass I would have been in the hospital. It was bad, y'all! So, so bad.

Heat helps me with pain, so I used a heating pad and took a hot bath and that helped some. I was able to sleep and woke up feeling decent again. Still grateful that I only had 4-5 oz and "green juice" is now on my "restricted" list!!

What is the plan now? Veggie broth is simmering on the stove and I will have that first. If that goes well, I'll add congee made with the same broth. Congee is a rice porridge made by boiling a small amount of rice in a large amount of water or broth until the rice breaks all the way down. It is delicious and soothing and always what I crave if I'm not feeling well. I also think it will be a very gentle way to reintroduce both rice and solids in general.

I will be adjusting my spreadsheet to start with the bland and beige foods and push veggies toward the end. Rough re-order will be something like broth, rice, chicken, oatmeal, fish, mashed potatoes, etc. This time though, I am just going to plan on needing to readjust as we go. Harder than the food bit is the mental part. I am going to stumble a lot as I work through this.

Becoming a Whipple Warrior

The hardest part of recovery is mental

As incredibly difficult as the physical part of this recovery has been, and continues to be, the mental part is probably the hardest part. I am struggling with anxiety and PTSD badly. "Regular" PTSD from my whipple and Complex PTSD from my abusive marriage. I sometimes feel depression starting to creep in but have thankfully been able to keep that beast away. This whole experience, from gallbladder to Whipple has been traumatic. Nothing has been in my control and it has all happened so fast. And getting divorced on top of everything. It is a lot.

I had what I like to refer to as a "Surprise Whipple." I went in expecting to have 3-hour ampullectomy and woke up after a 7+ hour Whipple. Yes, I knew there was a chance of the surgery converting, but it did not register that it was REALLY a possibility. I never even asked the obvious question of "if you do need to perform the Whipple, what is the recovery from that like?" Did not occur to me.

My very first memory after the surgery, when I was still in recover is a vivid one. My eyes were still closed and had not opened yet. I was just beginning to come back around but was not fully awake yet. I had this image in my head of the recovery area being like something I once saw on TV with rows of beds next to each other. I heard the word "Whipple." I do not remember any other words, just "Whipple." I clearly remember hearing that word and thinking "I wonder who had a Whipple. I sure hope it wasn't me!" I do not even remember when I was actually told I'd had a Whipple. I just remember the first time I heard the word and thinking the doctor was talking about someone else.

I had googled Whipple before my surgery but didn't really dig into it. The possibilities as my surgeon laid them out, knowing that you cannot really know for sure until you are open on the table AND pathology comes back, were as follows:

➢ Ampullectomy goes as planned and just that one small part of the ampula of vadar is removed

➢ If the pathology shows that he cannot get enough margin, he would need to convert to the Whipple (pathology is done DURING surgery and preliminary results are returned during the surgery)

➢ Presuming the ampullectomy, if the deeper pathology came back showing cancer or unclear margins, he's go back in after 2-3 days to perform the Whipple

➢ If my symptoms did not improve after the ampullectomy, I would need the Whipple 4-6 months down the road

Now that is a LOT of scenarios where I would be getting a Whipple so that should have been my first sign that I needed to take it seriously. I assumed I'd be lucky and everything would go as planned. Boy am I learning the hard lesson that things do not always go as planned!!! In hindsight, I think my brain shut down on March 19th when Dr. Obideen told me that the biopsy he took showed the pre-cancerous ampullory adenoma and that it would need to be surgically removed very quickly. I thought I was thinking clearly and asking the right questions and retaining information. I was not. Not even close!
Suffice it to say, I was quite ill prepared for dealing with recovery from a Whipple. I had NO IDEA until 2 months post-Whipple that there are challenges I will very likely struggle with for LIFE. I had no idea the kind of changes I would need to make to my diet and lifestyle. And no idea that these changes would not be optional. It is a lot to process and take it. It breeds anxiety over 'messing up'

because mess ups could mean severe pain, or another stay in the hospital. The stakes are just so much higher now. That is a lot of pressure! Also, there is no magic formula, and everyone is different so it's a lot of painful trial and error. Eating is now a game of Russian roulette and that can be terrifying.

Food is so social!

One of the most frustrating things I am working on is the realization of just how much foot is tied to socialization and relationships. Everything seems to revolve around food!! Everything seems to include a meal. At work, a lot of the socialization happens over lunch. Girls nights always involve food (and wine!). Holidays all have a specific set of foods.

It all becomes so much more noticeable when you either a) cannot eat, or b) cannot eat a full meal, c) can only eat a specific set of foods, prepared in a specific way, and d) need to be close to a bathroom or home after eating. I thought eating out was hard when I was vegan! Hahahahaha...vegans ain't got nuthin' on this Whippler!

So far, I've been able to avoid most work lunches. There are a select few who understand my new challenges so I can enjoy lunches with them without feeling super awkward. I guess I am mostly nervous for the inevitable lunch or lunch meeting with those who will not understand and give me considerable side eye for not eating much, or at all. I am already getting a lot of pressure to "just eat" because my weight is still dropping as I figure this out. By the way, that is SUPER unhelpful and makes me feel pretty terrible.

The last thing I want to touch on is eating with the family. While I still sit at family dinners, it is so hard to not be able to enjoy a full meal. I also worry about the message that limited portions send to my developing children. They all eat much more than I do! Even my 3-year-old! I try to talk to them a lot and be really open about what happened to Mummy, about my Whipple, and why I need to eat differently, little but often. Also, why their nutritional needs are different. All without scaring them that this could happen to them. Since my genetic tests came back clean the odds of them getting what I got and having a Whipple is extremely small. Still, it is tough.

I made a quick list of ideas for social things that do not include food:

- Hiking/walking
- Swimming
- Paint your own pottery
- Goodwill treasure hunting
- Book club
- Go to a park
- Museums
- Aquarium
- Movies
- Camping
- Bonfire
- Theater
- Comedy Club
- Game night
- Craft night
- Spa – Mani/Pedi

14 Weeks Status

Today I am 14 weeks out from my Whipple, and I'm so grateful to be there! The first 2 months were HELL. The 3rd month gave me hope of returning to some semblance of a life worth living. The 4th month is showing me that life can be great again!

I've had many struggles throughout this recovery and expect to have many more. The one I am currently working on is food and getting some healthy weight back on (or even just to stabilize my weight where it is! I am now down 25 lbs since my Whipple (and 193 lbs overall!) and am bouncing back from an "angry pancreas" episode.

Post flare I was fasting for a few days before trying to reintroduce food. I started wrong and had a, thankfully, short lived, flare. I have now been successful with veggie broth and rice (all organic, and all homemade). I am also up .2 lbs from yesterday so I'm thrilled to have at least stabilized my weight, as I'd been steadily losing for the past week or so. I'm now getting nutrition in every 1.5 – 2 hrs and will add a new food tomorrow, and every 2 days. The wrong foods or wrong amounts can trigger a flare up. A flare up can escalate into full blown pancreatitis so it is important to stop is early.

I have gotten a lot of grief about the fasting part since I'm already thin and losing and need the nutrition so wanted to explain. Here is the medical reason for it. When your pancreas gets angry, it gets inflamed. Inflammation causes swelling. That swelling makes is awfully hard for the digestive enzymes it produces to flow out to my intestines.

Said enzymes, when they cannot get out, start digesting the pancreas. It can cause sepsis and internal bleeding and can kill you. Very, very painful! Did you know that pancreatitis has a 10% fatality rate? Yeah, neither did I! To stop the pancreas from producing enzymes (and thus digesting itself), you must stop eating until the inflammation and swelling subside. Clear liquids are the name of the game.

Starting tomorrow the plan is to add back egg whites. This will give me a protein boost without experimenting with fats quite yet. They are also bland and easy to digest. Tougher foods and fiber will wait a little bit. I am committed to going slow and adding new foods every 2 days or so. The goal is to both build up the list of "safe" foods, as well as identify any that give me trouble so I can avoid them. Any of the foods that give me trouble will get rested again farther down the road as my body adapts to its new digestive system.

Food aside, my energy has been good and I am now up to walking a little over 3 miles at a time! I am still slow, and I am not really walking for a "workout" so I'm pretty happy with it. It is nice to get outside, enjoy the beautiful scenery around me, and not give a care in the world to heart rate or calories burned like I used to. I wave and talk to the cows, horses, alpacas, pigs, chickens, goats, bull, donkey, and ducks I get to see! How lucky am I to have all those animals to see on such short walks?!

I can do more with the kids now and have been cooking more. Even starting to feel up to a little closet organizing very soon! I have been sitting in the sun and floating around in the pool. I never really took the time to relax before and it is AMAZING!

Perspective and gratitude

Perspective makes all the difference in life. I have always known this, but over the past few months I have experienced such a profound shift in perspective that it often catches me off guard. The things that I now consider important are quite different, as are the things I choose to focus on. And choose is maybe not quite the right word because it is so natural it doesn't feel like it could even be another way. Instead of waxing poetic I wanted to simply list a few I have been hyper aware of lately.

New/Different Perspectives:
- ➢ I do not sweat the small stuff...and most everything is small stuff. I used to try to do everything and be perfect at everything. I had the perpetual need to be busy to feel justified...for what, I am not even sure anymore. Now, the only things that matter are connections & kindness. Everything that is important is some version of one of those two.

- ➢ I am simply not competitive anymore. Where you are versus where I am just does not matter. Life is not a race and our goals, desires, passions are so different that what is a "win" for you may not even register as important for me.

- ➢ I actively choose my perspective and I choose to: Always, always assume good intent and always, always assume that everyone is doing the absolute best they can on their journey. Never take things personally, even when someone tries to make it personal. You always have the power to choose your response. Choose kindness and compassion. Always.

➢ Always be grateful for struggles, setbacks, and challenges. This is where you learn. You will learn just how strong you are. You will learn how to overcome hard things. You will have the opportunity to empathize and help others

I'm so Grateful for:

➢ I am alive

➢ I survived one of the most brutal surgeries that exists and am stronger for it! And am grateful that it was even an option for me!

➢ I have a wonderful and amazing kiddos

➢ I have wonderful neighbors and friends

➢ I have had the opportunity to learn more about the human body and it is a fascinatingly complex miracle

➢ I am learning a new perspective on food and how to use food as fuel and medicine

➢ I am learning how to socialize less around food and with more focus on connection and new experiences

➢ My children are learning about compassion, care taking, healthy eating, and pulling together as a family

➢ I have an utterly amazing work family that have been so supportive of my time away and continued recovery

➢ I am alive!

Food and supplements

First, a quick update of my eating situation. In short, I am doing great and eating 7-10 times per day! Granted it is still just a few bites at a time, but it is sitting well, causing no pain or discomfort, and it's getting my body re accustomed to food and a very regular schedule of it! So far, I have had veggie broth, white and brown rice, and egg whites (hooray for getting protein back!). Today I am trying nonfat plain Greek yogurt then tomorrow or Friday I am going to add some soft, white fish next for even more protein. Over the weekend I will start with some soft cooked green beans and go from there. My weight is also holding steady which is great!

Now, supplements. I do take quite a few and feel noticeably better when I do so want to share what I've chosen to take and why. Granted I have no scientific evidence that I feel better because they work, or if I feel better because I *think* they work. Either way, I feel better! I will also add then anytime I am not feeling well or have angered my pancreas, I tend to stop any supplements just in case.

Here is what I currently take, along with a solid multivitamin and extra vitamin C.

➢ Turmeric: It is a powerful anti-inflammatory and antioxidant. I get inflammation very quickly and easily and so this one makes sense for me. I use it in cooking a lot too!

➢ Grape Seed Extract: Helps with poor circulation and can reduce swelling (surgery causes swelling)! It is also high in antioxidants. I have Reynaud's syndrome and experience cold hands/feet due to poor circulation and this helps that, in addition to helping reduce swelling that is still lingering in my abdominal area from surgery.

➢ Probiotics: For a healthy gut bacteria and improved digestion.

➢ Biotin: Not technically enough data here to support its use, but I am taking it because I started losing a TREMENDOUS amount of hair with the trauma and anesthesia from so much surgery. Whether it would have slowed anyway or not, it absolutely slowed down once I started supplementing.

➢ Collagen: Has many benefits, but I take it to help build muscle back that I lost, the digestive health benefits, organ protection, and of course the skin elasticity benefits (I am not getting any younger!).

➢ COQ10: Helps produce energy in your cells and decreases with age, and the big one for me is that by reducing oxidative stress in the body it is thought that it may play a role in cancer prevention.

Yet to try, but I have them:

➢ Noni Fruit: Polynesian healers have used noni fruits for thousands of years to help treat a variety of health problems. I am interested in it for its anti-inflammation benefits as well as its anti tumor/cancer benefits (by way of stimulating the production of nitric oxide). It is also said to be antibacterial, antifungal, antiviral; helps with IBS/constipation, skin/hair benefits, and as a natural immune booster.

➢ Medicinal Mushrooms (reishi, lion's mane, chaga, shitake, turkey tail, cordyceps): Click to learn about each of these mushrooms, but there are many apparent benefits for your brain, hormones, and immune system). Reishi in particular is supposed to help with healing.

➢ Bosweillia (Indian Frankincense): This is another one for inflammation, as well as for arthritis, asthma, and IBS/digestion support. It has been used for centuries in Asian and African medicine.

Of course, it goes without saying, but please speak with your doctor about any supplements you take or are considering taking.

Dairy is a "no" at the moment

Overall, the "slow re-entry" diet is going well, and I am eating 8-10 times per day. Small amounts, but it has been good to get a steady stream of nutrition in! The biggest thing I have learned so far is that I may not be as OK with dairy as I had thought or assumed. I have struggled with massive bloating for an awfully long time now. The kind of bloating that makes me look pregnant and show up dramatically on the scale. Not as real weight, but as retained fluids.

I was chugging along doing well with veggie broth, brown and white rice, and egg whites. Then I added 8 oz of non-fat plain Greek yogurt spread across the day. I started having some abdominal pain to the point I pulled out the "big guns" of abdominal binders for relief. Then I started noticing my belly poking out. The bloat! I still did not associate it with the yogurt. Not sure why it did not occur to me since I am intentionally doing a slow re-entry diet to uncover food reactions exactly like this! It only clicked when I woke up to a 1.5-pound weight gain...when I have been running on a serious calorie deficit. Then it hit me – yogurt makes me tummy hurt and makes me bloat!!

I am hoping it is not all dairy, but I stopped the yogurt and will let it clear my system for a day before trying a different food. I will try dairy again, but it feels very satisfying (though frustrating) to have learned something valuable!

Bottom line is that this is hard and slow, but it is working. Also, my energy is soaring from being able to eat so often, even if I'm still working up to the right number of calories!

Investing in health!

I have been through a lot this year. So have my kids and my mother. While all the medical issues this year were physically mine, they greatly impacted and affected the entire family. It has been very difficult, but not without bright spots, lessons learned, shifts in priorities, and a strong focus on how we invest out time, money, and resources.

One of our big focus areas is health. Surely this is not a surprise to anyone reading this and it has always been important to me. My brush with cancer was a little too close for comfort this year. Then learning that I have zero genetic predispositions to any cancers, our focus became even more important. While it is always a random thing, there is certainly a connection between exposure of toxic things and cancer. I want to reduce our exposure as much as possible!

What does that mean? It means that I look for products that are natural, homemade, free from toxic chemicals, organic, and non-GMO. It's little things like using a citrus infused vinegar as my all-purpose cleaner or switching to safer skincare/sunscreen/makeup products, like Beautycounter.

A huge part of it is FOOD! As you know, my world pretty much revolves around food...what I can eat, cannot eat, how much, when, etc. I want to be sure that what we eat, what we put in our bodies is as clean and chemical free as possible. I am so excited that we are able to source excellent produce from a local farm that uses organic practices. Today we got out first basket and it is AMAZING! Full of corn, tomatoes, squash, cucumbers, beans, and okra – delicious!!

We have 2 bench freezers, a dehydrator, a foodsaver, and a pressure canner. What we cannot eat fresh, we can preserve to enjoy all year long! This weekend I will be both pickling and dehydrating okra!

About that time "I saw the Light" and "met God"

I have been debating whether to share this part of my Whipple journey. It is both very personal, and probably a bit controversial too. I ultimately decided to share because it just felt right. I am not sure if there is maybe someone who needs to read this today, or if there is some other reason, but today felt like the right time. I know I will never find the word to do this experience justice so bear with me.

I want to preface by being open about the fact that I am not a religious person. I am not a Christian. I do not attend church. I do not believe in doctrine, and I do not see the bible, or any other religious texts as anything other than historical and/or political documents. I have zero judgement and the utmost respect for anyone who has different beliefs. I have always agreed with the statement that if you use your religion to judge or justify mistreatment or lack of respect for others, you are doing it wrong.

I am, however, a very spiritual person. What I mean by that is that I believe we are all connected and that the concept of that ultimate connection is maybe what religions mean by "God" in any case. I believe all religions fundamentally come down to one thing at their core: LOVE. If I had to identify with any religion, I'd say Buddhism resonates most with me. Probably because it is not a religion, it is a practice. You can BE Catholic/Jewish/Muslim, etc. and still PRACTICE Buddhism. Buddhism comes down to 2 things (which both = love): 1)

Treat others with loving kindness, and 2) Do no harm. That just feels right to me.

I have always suspected there is some kind of fairly universal experience that people have, regardless of religion, spirituality, or belief, when death is near. Whether it is a near death experience, or a final death. I will also add that I believe how our brains work probably contributes to this. There are just so many strikingly similar stories of people who "see the light" and come back that it just feels universal. I guess this one will have to remain a mystery to the living.

My experience was indeed quite like the stories I've read. Maybe just hearing the stories influences the experience? It was clear, real, and overwhelming in any case. I was in the hospital after my Whipple surgery and in an extreme amount of pain. My epidural had slipped out of place and the pain was not well controlled. I did not know at the time that I would experience pain much more severe as I proceeded through recovery. Would not have thought it was even possible! It was still incredibly intense and not a pain I could even describe other than saying it was the kind of pain you did not think you could survive and felt like it would never end.

I was barely awake/conscious, and I remember closing my eyes and seeing an incredibly intense light that was both fantastically bright, yet soothing and reassuring and warm at the same time. It was the pure embodiment of love. I cannot describe it any other way. It was just love. Pure and complete love. Like the veil between worlds was lifted and I was seeing to the other side.

It was also very clearly a choice for me. I did not see a figure or hear any words in a physical way. It was just a knowing. I knew, sure as I am sitting here today, that if I wanted to leave this physical world/plane behind, all I needed to do was keep my eyes closed and I would make the transition. I struggled to open them, then close them again to "shake" this off. Yet every time I closed my eyes again, which I did 3 times, it was still there.

One the second time I kept them closed the longest. It was during this time that I heard/was told very clearly that "it is your choice to stay or move on" and the other things I got was "let him go. He is not for you." I knew this was about my now ex-husband. It was not a physical voice but a deep down 'knowing.' It is hard to adequately describe.

I felt sucked in and the lure to keep my eyes closed and just be enveloped in that love light was incredibly strong. As my eyes were closed, I thought of my children especially and forced my eyes open. If not for them, I 100% for sure would have given in.

It has never left me that I am here because of a choice I made. There were so many times earlier in my recovery where I wanted to give up. I could not see an end to the pain and agony I was in. To call this surgery brutal just does not even seem to scratch the surface. There are no words that are substantial enough to do this experience justice. And only I will ever really know just how bad it was. Or that, even though I "look great" and am doing a lot more normal things now, I still struggle mightily. Daily. I work ridiculously hard to focus on the positive and to keep an optimistic outlook, which I believe is helping my recovery. Thought I am sure that focus often gives the impression that things are back to normal and that I am recovered now. They are not and I am not. Better, yes. Back to normal and recovered, no. There is still a long road ahead of me.

My "seeing the light" experience is something I could also describe as "meeting God." Except that I do not really like the word God. God sounds like an individual person to me and for me, the concept of God is the embodiment of the connection we ALL have. I believe that this connection is what is being referred to when I hear things like "God is a part of all of us." I am not sure those are the right words, but that general idea that we are all God and God is all of us.

One thing this experience has taught me is that while I used to get stuck on and aggravated by certain religion-based words and ideas and how they are expressed, I just don't anymore. It just does not matter to me anymore what words people use to describe their beliefs, or even what those beliefs are. I think that everyone connects with the words, beliefs, and actions that resonate with them and so long as the focus is on love, the rest does not matter. Whereas before I would never use the words "God" or "pray" (and frankly, did not even like when people said they'd pray for me), now I am apt to use whatever words resonate with OTHER people, regardless of if they resonate with me. It just feels so silly to have ever focused on a word.

For me, prayer is simply calling on that connection we all have because what is good for one of us is good for the entire connected being. I believe that setting intentions is incredibly powerful and that when there are larger collections of individuals focusing on the same intention (praying), change can and does happen. I had a LOT of people praying for me and it very clearly worked and it something I am incredibly grateful for! While my recovery has been very rough, I am still doing so much better than so many people and there is simply no other reason for it.

So, thank you for your prayers, and yes, I will pray for you too. Even though the words or method may be different, I hope the result of filling the universe with loving intent will still be the same.

Whipple attack at work and total exhaustion

After many, many good days, today was completely rotten. I was exhausted last night and went to bed early. I slept solid for well over 9 hours and still struggled hard to get up. The exhaustion was so complete it was like a physical weight on me.

I made it into the office and even after coffee and some B vitamins I was still just as exhausted. Then, as I pulled into my parking spot, I felt a whipple attack coming on. Thank goodness I get some 'warning' time first! The pain started building and I had to sit in my car for several minutes before I could move. I managed to make it into the building and to a private bathroom where I had to lie on the floor in a fetal position to get through the pain. It was awful.

Whipple attacks always leave me exhausted and this one was no different. I am thankful this was only one attack and not four like last time!! The rest of the day was a double whammy of exhaustion so thick I could barely function.

I made it through my meetings and drove home around 3:30 when they ended. I went immediately to bed and slept solid for a couple more hours before getting up to get the kids to bed. I plan to go back to bed after a cup of hot tea.

Best I can figure I brought this on myself by walking a full 5 miles on Sunday after walking 3 the previous day. I was tired but ok Monday and today it just caught up with me.

Even though the intensity of my walks is incredibly low, apparently distance and time matter right now. I expect to feel good again tomorrow but will probably wait until Thursday or even Friday to walk again. Recovery just takes me a lot longer these days.

So, I am still learning and unfortunately, learning the hard way more than I would like. It is easy to feel more ok than I am and then overdo it. I need to remember that and pace myself more.

Feeling good again!

Looks like rest is my best medicine right now. My Mom shared the wise notion that perhaps it is when I am feeling good that I most need to remember to pace myself and rest. She is right. Per usual. It is easy to not do too much when I am not feeling well. When I am feeling good, I tend to just go for it. Often with abandon. Often that gets me in trouble – oops!

I have found that, reliably, when I overdo it I take about 4 days to get totally back to where I was. Yesterday was 4 days so today I plan to walk on the treadmill at the company gym. By the way, how AMAZING is it that I have a company gym to use?! I am going to take it slow and easy and stick to my 3.1 miles which I know is exactly right for me at the moment. I will take it easy Saturday and walk again Sunday.

I am eating a bit better now too! I can have small amounts (portions are KEY for me!!) of rice, chicken, lamb, pasta with red sauce, string cheese, tortilla chips, and I even did ok with a spinach artichoke dip with Greek yogurt! Last I had Greek yogurt it HATED me, and I bloated up to about a 6 month pregnant size. I spaced out and forgot and got the spinach artichoke dip made with the Greek yogurt ON PURPOSE (because I forgot – anesthesia brain fog is REAL and lasts forever!) because it was lower in fat.

It would be super nice if foods gave me more reliable reactions though. Feels very out of control to have a bad reaction one day then no reaction another. Hard to pinpoint true causes. There probably is not one though.

My system is still just relearning how to process and digest food so that takes time. This is another reason that small portions are key is that it limits the severity of any reactions. Also, I am missing part of my stomach, so I get full super-fast anyway.

That is pretty much it. I had an overall great week at work (except that one bad day), and it was my most productive since returning which felt great! I am looking forward to spending some quality time with my kids this weekend and with a few other families for an "end of summer" pool party and cookout before school starts for many next week.

Sick and Missing Out

Yesterday was so fun! Took the kids to the Canton Farmers Market where we saw friends, loaded up on fresh produce and baked treats, and had some delicious food. Bear & Elara got their faces painted too!

We had carnitas and tomato sandwiches – super delicious!! However, two things I CANNOT have are apparently pork (should have learned my lesson from 4th of July!!) and tomatoes. I have been incredibly sick, in pain, and in bed for over 24 hrs now. I am about to miss our "end of summer" pool party and cookout that starts in less than an hour.

I am so sick of getting so sick!! This episode is lasting a lot longer than usual and I am just so over it. Probably because I started not feeling well Friday and in hindsight, should have switched to a liquid diet for a day instead of enjoying our farmers market bounty. It is my own fault though. I knew better. I am just so frustrated by not being able to eat normally anymore.

Ok, pity party should be winding down soon. I am hoping to feel better by tomorrow, or even this evening. I am just so weak and dehydrated on top of the pain that I'll likely stay in bed until morning. Blerg!

An Emotional Week

It has been a very emotional week. I have cried, yelled, and just collapsed into exhausted sleep. I cannot see an ambulance with lights and sirens and not break down from the memories of being in so many of them this year. Let me back up a little. I started having an increasing pain around my "upper right quadrant" that was wrapping around to my back. Classic pancreas pain. This was a little different though in that there it was also a specific, dull stabbing pain over my side as well that would not budge.

Assuming it was "just" another pancreas flare up, I put myself on "clears" starting Sunday afternoon, which is basically fasting with clear liquids. The reason for this is to give my pancreas a break and let the inflammation goes down. When the pancreas gets inflamed, it swells, and the digestive enzymes cannot get out. The release of digestive enzymes is triggered when you eat only. My pancreatic duct is significantly smaller than normal, so it takes very little to swell it shut. When they cannot get out, they go back into the pancreas and it starts basically digesting itself, which can lead to necrosis and sepsis and even death. Scary stuff!

It was still bad on Monday and I called my surgeon to see what I should do. I was in so much pain I had packed my contacts, phone charger, and hospital socks because I was fairly sure I was going to be sent to the ER then admitted. It was that bad on Monday. I didn't' get a call back until late in the day and we decided I'd head in Tuesday morning for labs and an appointment. Fasting that whole day was helping some and since I have still got a fair amount of anxiety about ERs and hospitals that was fine with me. My pain was at a solid 5-6.

My labs looked ok. No pancreatitis which was a relief! I did learn that I will always need to supplement with B12, calcium, and vitamin D, and the labs did show that I had not been getting adequate nutrition recently, which was not a big surprise. My surgeon is thorough and amazing, and they decided to do a CT scan anyway just to be sure we weren't missing anything. I was in for labs, my appointment, and finished the CT scan in time to be back at work at 2 pm – impressive! I assumed the CT would be completely clear and did not think much else of it.

Wednesday I got a call from the surgeon's office and learned that while the CT was clear from a surgical perspective (nothing Whipple related), they did find something called an adnexal cyst on the left side (exactly where my pain was, and still is). I believe it is like an ovarian cyst. The recommendation was to get into a gynecologist ASAP to confirm, hopefully, that it is benign and not something scary like ovarian cancer. So, I am terrified now. Then my gyno cannot fit me in until SEPTEMBER 30th! I lost it. Just started crying right there on the phone.

Thank the stars above that I have amazing friends and I was able to get in with one of the TOP gynecologists in Atlanta next Thursday! So, I am getting my CT scan and labs transferred over to the new gyno and I feel much better about being able to get seen sooner than later. I am sure it's nothing, but it's scary after everything else this year. And honestly, if they recommend any kind of surgery to remove it, I'm just going to ask for a full hysterectomy so I don't ever have to worry about ovarian cancer! Might as well – I've already hit all of my out-of-pocket maximums and deductibles this year!

When I was finally seen, it turned out to be an ovarian cyst related to my cycle. Goodie! Though not dangerous, my doctor decided that with all I had been through already this year I should not also have to deal with the anxiety this kind of pain could cause.

Thankfully, the fix was as simple as hormonal birth control. Since we were unsure about my absorption due to the whipple, I got a vaginal ring. It fixed the issue, and more than a year later, still no more cysts!

Post-Whipple: Months 6-18 months

This part is being written about 18 months after my Whipple. I stopped blogging and got off all social media about 6 months pos-Whipple because I was also going through an exceedingly difficult, and long overdue divorce. I regret not blogging or journaling the ups and downs of it all, but I was simply unable to at the time. I was in pure survival mode. I did survive though!

I have steadily improved and recovered day by day. Food is still a struggle and I cannot tolerate too much sugar or carbs. I do have them more now though, but still need to be careful, especially with sugar. I do better with dairy, but it will still give me issues if I have too much at a time. At this point though, I can really eat anything I want, so long as I do not have too much of the things higher in sugars, carbs, or fats. There is hope! You CAN eat normally post-whipple. It just takes time.

I will still get random Whipple attacks, usually brough on by stress or sugar. I know how to manage them by with rest and a diet of "clears" for a few days. Learning that stress can bring them on has been very eye opening!

Oh the Emotions!

The biggest changes and challenges throughout this journey have been emotional. My Whipple was in April of 2019. I asked for a divorce in August 2019 (after also asking for one in the summer of 2018), I moved out in December 2019, had my ex served after he refused to settle amicably in January of 2020, and the divorce was finally finalized in August of 2020. Oh, and let us not forget the global pandemic that began in March of 2020 and that I got laid off the same week I got divorced. So, I have been recovering from one of the world's most complex surgeries while navigating a nasty divorce involving my 4 amazing children in the middle of a global pandemic. We are all ok, but it is hard.

I will not make this book about the divorce, but I will say that trying to recover physically from something this extreme, while also trying to recover from a tremendous amount of trauma makes things so much harder. I believe in my core that a lot of the issues that led to me needing a Whipple in the first place came, at least in part, from trying to handle so much trauma while trying to also appear "fine" on the outside and for everyone else. We hold emotional trauma and pain in our bodies and the more extreme the trauma, the more it will be held in the body. I know there has been research on this, but this is just my opinion based on my own personal experiences.

Since I was dealing with so much emotionally and mentally, I did a staggering amount of therapy. I highly suggest that if you live on this earth, you should have an amazing therapist. Mine has been such a life saver and I am so thankful for her. I am an empath and having a therapist who is also an empath and understands how I process the world has been nothing short of divine.

I have been learning to care for myself and heal myself. Everyone's journey here will be different so I will not share my details here and now, but I wouldn't be here if I did not have the support of an amazing therapist, my mother, children, and a great group of friends. When you go through something as intense as this surgery and divorce, you really find out who your true friends are. Not the people only there when things are fun, but those willing to get down in the hole with you and support you and love you until you can dig yourself out.

The farther out from my traumas I get the more my complex PTSD is kicking in. I am working on it, but it is a struggle every day. I am being open in sharing my triggers with those around me, so they know how to be patient with me and support me. I am also getting a golden retriever puppy soon that, with help from professionals, I will be training as a service dog to aid me with the CPTSD symptoms like extreme anxiety, flashbacks, nightmares, and more. Sometimes even (or especially?) you do not realize how bad a situation was until you are safely out. I am grateful that I am out, safe, healing, and moving on with an amazing life! I am grateful that surviving the whipple gave me the courage to know I can survive and thrive through anything.

One of the other things I have been doing as part of my therapy is getting back to my Reiki practice. Reiki is a form of energy healing. I am a Reiki master and sound healer and often forget to use it for myself. I hit a point in my recovery where I "remembered" that I have a documented (by medical professionals) history of healing myself with Reiki.

I started doing regular and focused Reiki sessions mixed with intensive visualization for myself. I was focusing on healing my pancreas to produce more enzymes on my own so I could be less reliant on my prescription enzymes and feel better. It took me 2-3 months, but I have been able to significantly reduce the amount of enzymes I need to take and overall feel so much better. I've even been able to put some much-needed weight back on! I am now close to my pre-surgery weight and thrilled about it!

Along with Reiki and visualization, I also restarted my daily meditation practice. That helped with my emotional healing more than anything. It helped me refocus on myself and helped me rediscover who I am. It helps me keep focused on the truth of who I am and not so much on who anxiety says I am. I highly recommend it! You can start small by simply closing your eyes and breathing.

Hair Loss...

One of the effects of the surgery that did not happen until a bit later was hair loss. I was completely unprepared for this! I did not have chemo, or anything so did not even think this was a possibility. Apparently, a lot of anesthesia can cause hair loss. Also, when your body is recovering from something this massive all your energy goes into that recovery. So, less resources available for growing hair.

All told I estimate that I lost a solid 70% of my hair. It just got super thin and stringy. I eventually chose to cut it all off and get a pixie! I was terrified, having had long hair my entire life, but it was incredibly empowering, and I am so glad I did it! My hair is still growing back, but I love it and it is so much thicker and healthier, and my curls are even looking better!

I mention this so you can be prepared if you are undergoing this, or any major surgery. Maybe it will not happen and that is amazing. But if it does, know it is normal and it is just hair so have some fun with a short cut! As a woman it also brought up just how much female identity is tied up in long hair. I think that is why cutting it was so empowering for it. It was my way of reclaiming ME. Of doing something just for me and nobody else.

Poop & Toots!

In a not so smooth transition, another thing to be aware of post-whipple is poop. And flatulence. You will forever be examining your poop to know if you are absorbing nutrients and if things are going well, digestively. Every doctor appointment will have questions about poop. You will also have some of the most foul-smelling poop you can even imagine. What you do not want to see: light colored poops, poops that float, or oil floating in the toilet. All signs you are not absorbing your nutrients and may need more enzymes. Fun stuff!

Oh, and flatulence. My kids call them "whipple toots." I do not have gas often but if I eat something wrong or eat too much, lord have mercy can I ever clear a room! Seriously, it is awful. I have cancelled plans over it. Nothing to be done but let whatever I had that disagreed with me work its' way on through my system.

Taking the enzymes helps, but poop and toots will forever be an issue. At least that is what I am anticipating. I feel like at 18 months out things are relatively stable now. I feel good, my scar is amazing, and I can, for the most part, eat normally. Though I can still feel tugging at the incision site if I try and lift something too heavy.

Speaking of lifting, I should probably be doing a lot more weight training than I do. I am back to full activity and mostly walk, hike, do the elliptical, or spin bike. For strength I stick with yoga, Pilates, and body weight things like planks. Walking has proven very help for digestion.

Just my theory but I think that moving helps food make its way through my system, so I digest things better.

At 18 months out, I feel good saying that I feel recovered. I still have off days with food or a little pain, and still have the occasional whipple attack. It all feels more settled and normal now. Stable. More predictable. Manageable. I no longer feel like I will be forever enveloped in whipple issues. My life is mostly normal now, only more badass for being such an awesome survivor!

Have hope. Take it one day at a time. Trust that you will feel good again. Know that better things are right around the corner. You've got this!

Hospital Items I Loved

I wanted to share some of the items I found to be particularly helpful for me both in the hospital and at home as I recovered from my Whipple. Everyone is different and this is just my experience. Hopefully, it will be helpful.

- ➢ 2 small toddler pillows were helpful for propping my arms, behind my head, and later to support my stomach for sleeping. Also very helpful for holding against my incision for coughing and sneezing!

- ➢ I LOVE my "Mattress Genie" which is an inflatable, button controlled, bed wedge that made getting comfortable and in and out of bed easier. Later on, it's great for reading or watching TV in bed, or when you need your head elevated for a cold! (Bed Bath & Beyond may be cheaper with their coupons!)

- ➢ A hospital style adjustable table for beside the bed or recliner was perfect! I was unable to reach around or behind me to my regular bedside table. This was handy for medications, drinks, meals, anything I needed to have handy. Great later as a laptop table to work from!

- ➢ A recliner!! We have an old manual one and I needed help at first to recline it and sit it back up. If you can swing it, get an automatic push button one!

- ➢ You may lose a lot of weight after your Whipple and when that happens a lot of us lose our bums! This makes sitting right on the tailbone very painful. A coccyx pillow is now a MUST for me now. I have one at home, one in my car, and one at the office.

➢ Not a necessity by any stretch, but I loved having my own hospital gown that fit and were cute!! I even monogrammed mine. I looked up maternity hospital

 gowns on amazon to find mine.

➢ Also, not necessary but I loved my cute non-slip yoga socks...MUCH nicer than the hospital grippy socks! Those do not fit well at all and they WILL require you to wear non-slip socks for walking...and you WILL be walking.

➢ Nightshirts for home because at first, pulling down your pants to use the bathroom will be hard. There may also be some 'urgent' situations where you will not want pants to slow you down!

➢ Lip balm & hair ties!

➢ Pretty blankets/throws just to give you a little joy! I chose flamingos as my 'recovery theme' and I loved my flamingo Sherpa blanket!

➢ An abdominal binder or compression tank. Your organs we just massively shifted around, and it feels, well, weird! Some days I did not want anything touching my stomach. Some days I needed compression to feel 'put together.' I got a few different binders from Amazon to try, as well as some body sharper style compression tanks from TJMaxx. You may need to experiment with what works for you. I still, 18 months later, wear a compression tank under pretty much everything. It just feels better.

➢ A pre-stocked pantry with gentle foods to get your started as you figure out what you tolerate best. For me it was bone broth, cottage cheese, yogurt, canned green beans, cream of rice cereal, rice, applesauce, pudding, protein shakes, blueberries

➤ A list of shows and movies to watch! I spent the better part of 8 weeks in bed and watched shows when I was up for it (I was not for quite some time!) and watched until I never wanted to see another TV again! Reading physical books was physically hard and I would fall asleep with audio books and kept losing my place. Mostly I napped, but when I needed shows it was good to know what I wanted to watch!

The End Part...

Am I Thriving?

What a crazy rollercoaster the past year and a half has been! When I look back, it is often hard to comprehend just how much I survived. Surviving is one thing. Thriving is another. My goal is always to take every experience and learn, grow, evolve, and THRIVE! I would say yes, I am thriving! Does that mean I do not still have very difficult days and challenging times? Absolutely not. I have, however, learned how to better manage all challenges life throws my way. Thriving will look different for everyone. For me it looks like good medical health. I am recovered to the point where my surgery is not a daily thought. I am physically healed and have a normal and healthy relationship with food. I am nourished and don't experience more than the normal digestive distress. For the most part. Am I still careful about what I eat? Of course. But I would be careful regardless of any surgery. There are still foods that cause me issues, but that was true before the surgery too. Thriving also looks like good mental and emotional health. I have worked so hard to process all of my traumas and gain new coping techniques, like meditation, breathing, walking, and simple self-care on a consistent basis. I now stand firmly in the knowledge that I have inherent value as a person, regardless of my contributions to invididuals or organization. I treat myself with love and care, as I would anyone I love. Through surviving my whipple, I found the strength to leave an abusive situation. While I am still working through the aftermath of that trauma, I am safe and free and happy.

My children are doing well, and I am able to spend more quality one on one time with them without fear. I am being incredibly selective about what energies I allow in my space and am teaching my children to do the same. I know, set, and enforce healthy boundaries, and am teaching my children the same. I feel incredibly fortunate to have been gifted so many challenging situations to work through. It has taught me patience, perseverance, and so much more. As I work through my healing journey, which will never end, I am able to share information and tools for my children to do the same in their lives. I am able to give them a safe space to be loved and cherished and to express emotions and opinions and to practice boundary setting. As part of my journey to rediscover myself I am also learning and relearning all the things that make ME happy. I love to sing at the top of my lungs and dance around the kitchen. I adore a long hike in nature with nothing but my thoughts. Turns out I love, and am pretty good at, gardening! I have a huge passion for cooking. I am meeting new people and learning what non-toxic friendships and relationships look like. I am learning how I respond and feel in these new situations. It has been incredibly freeing and eye opening, and I feel like the whole world it at my feet to discover and enjoy! So yes. YES, I am absolutely THRIVING! You can too. Regardless of your situation and what you are facing, approach it with curiosity and as an opportunity to learn, grow, and evolve. And you absolutely will!

What Have I learned?

I was not sure what to call this part or how to wrap this up. "Conclusion" seems awfully formal and made it feel like a book report. I also do not think this story ever ends, though the acute part is over and that's what I wanted to write about.

I hope you have enjoyed my story and that there is at least one small nugget that will stick with you. I will wrap up with some of my biggest lessons from the past year:

➤ My track record for surviving hard things so far is 100%

➤ Never forget to treat yourself as well as you would treat someone you love

➤ Invest in a lot of therapy and be selective about the people you allow in your circle

➤ While the ability to prepare is wonderful, sometimes you just need to take things as they come and trust the process

➤ Get really comfortable with change and with things not going according to plan

➤ Do not get off the toilet during a colonoscopy prep once things have 'started.' You will poop on the floor.

➤ If you believe you can, you can. If you believe you can't, you can't. The mind is incredibly powerful – YOU are incredibly powerful.

➤ Follow your passions and do not worry if it's not perfect. Just start.

- ➤ Everything is temporary. The good and the bad. Enjoy the good. Turn the bad into lessons.

- ➤ Share your story – you never know who needs to hear it!

- ➤ Sometimes the éclair is worth the inevitable diarrhea and stinky toots

- ➤ Often when one door closes, it is because the whole world is about to open up for you

Love,
Kara

ACKNOWLEDGMENTS

I would not be healthy today if not for the heroic efforts of Dr. Kamil Obideen and Dr. Eddie Abdalla. The extraordinary level of care from these doctors and their staff and teams was truly astonishing. I'd like also especially thank Matt, Elaine, Anita, and Erica from Dr. Abdalla's office.

ABOUT THE AUTHOR

Kara Draper

is a single mother of 4 living in the Atlanta area. She is a graduate of Vanderbilt University where she studied psychology and political science. For her "day job" she helps technology organizations deliver on their highest return investments in the most efficient way possible. Kara is also a Reiki Master who does energy healing sessions for others and herself.

Kara is a survivor of numerous traumas and is navigating those experiences and her healing journey by sharing her stories. Her greatest desire is to give others hope, perspective, and even some helpful information as they navigate their own stories.

Made in the USA
Middletown, DE
06 February 2021